AT THE BEACH

At the BEACH

THE GREAT NEW ZEALAND HOLIDAY

Stephen Barnett and Richard Wolfe

Hodder & Stoughton
A member of the Hodder Headline Group

A Bookmakers Book
Edited, designed and produced by Bookmakers Design & Production Ltd
PO Box 46-120, Herne Bay, Auckland, New Zealand

© 1993 Stephen Barnett and Richard Wolfe

Excerpts © the sources acknowledged
Illustrations © the sources acknowledged on page 117
This arrangement © 1993 Bookmakers Design & Production Ltd

First published 1993 by Hodder & Stoughton Ltd
A division of Hodder Headline PLC
46 View Road, Glenfield, Auckland, New Zealand

ISBN 0 340 55488 6

Design and production by Stephen Barnett/Bookmakers
Typesetting by Hierographics, Auckland
Printed in Hong Kong

Front cover: photograph of caravanners at Goose Bay, Kaikoura, courtesy
Wilson & Horton Ltd. Pohutukawa illustration by Helen Humphries.
Page 6: 'On the Beach — New Brighton' by Grace Butler is reproduced by
kind permission of Mrs Grace Adams and the CSA Gallery, Christchurch.

This book is copyright. All rights reserved. No part of this publication may be reproduced or
transmitted in any form or by any means, electronic or mechanical, including photocopying,
recording, storage in any information retrieval system or otherwise, without the written
permission of the producer, Bookmakers Design & Production Ltd.

Contents

Introduction   7
The Lure of the Waves

TAKING THE PLUNGE   11
From the promenade and into the waves: the 'battle of the beach', mixed bathing, and surf life-saving.

PLEASURES OF THE PICNIC   29
A national institution: the Thermette and other accoutrements of the seaside repast, getting to the coast, beach accessories, the 'sound' of the beach, hanging five, beachcombing, and messing about in boats.

BEAUTY AND THE BEACH   53
From neck to knee: the evolution of the swimsuit, in and out of the sun, bathing belles, and beauty contests.

BESIDE THE SEASIDE   71
What we did in the holidays, our favourite beaches, hoping for a bite and other fishy tales, the bach, and under canvas.

Acknowledgements   117

Illustration Credits   117

Index   119

The Lure of the Waves
INTRODUCTION

THERE ARE MANY countries blessed with beaches where citizens escape for annual summer holidays. But, perhaps more than in any other country, enjoyment of New Zealand's extensive coastline is an all–year–round affair, an essential part of our lifestyle and popular culture. Access to these hundreds of fine beaches is our birthright.

In 1937 an enthusiastic writer claimed that New Zealand was 'unique in the whole wide world in its rich profusion of perfect bathing beaches'. With something of an oversight in respect of our wealth of black ironsand, we were labelled 'The Land of a Thousand Golden Beaches', possessors of a 'resplendent boon, of the best sea beaches to be found on the surface of the globe'. Such a wealth of choice makes it possible for there to be a beach for every situation. Beaches safe year-in and year-out for swimming, others with surfable waves or shallows for kids and dogs to splash about in. Trees for shade on hot sunny days when too much of a good thing drives beachgoers back from the exposed sands.

Some 6000 kilometres of coastline around a narrow landmass means that nowhere in New Zealand is far from the sea. The populace of all four of the traditional main centres — Auckland, Wellington, Christchurch and Dunedin — are only minutes removed from quality ocean beaches, while almost everyone else is, at worst, a couple of hours' drive away from one. (The residents of Garston in Southland must drive furthest — 130 kilometres — for a day at the beach.) It is on much of this coastline — along the Tasman and Pacific Oceans — that, in the words of one 1958 holiday guide, beachgoers can '. . . laze, alone or with a crowd, drifting between the hot sand, the warm sea and the soft shade of the crimson-blossomed pohutukawa trees'.

The story of New Zealanders and the beach is one that has its beginnings in the latter half of the last century. Up until then the beach had been largely

ignored as a place of recreation — rather, the waterfronts of our towns and cities were the preserves of those who earned their living from the sea. From around the middle of the 1870s, however, the country's city beaches in particular became increasingly favoured destinations for weekend promenades and picnics. Such rituals could be refreshed by the taking of tea at a pavilion or by listening to popular tunes at a band rotunda, but for the Victorians the sea was for looking at, not swimming in. Children might paddle, but adults for their part remained clothed and dry, not to mention hot!

In Britain, in the United States and in many of the countries of Europe at this time, 'sea-bathing' was already long established. Swimming in the sea would eventually be commonplace here, too, but not before it was first harried by the conventions of the times.

Along with golfing, tennis and cycling, swimming enjoyed in the 1880s the interest of a middle class that increasingly desired to spend part of its leisure time in sporting pursuits. At first, however, all swimming took place in public 'baths' provided by local councils . . . and with swimming strictly segregated.

It was inevitable, given the country's equable climate and the access by the great majority of its population to a wealth of fine beaches, that 'sea bathing' should be the next step. How this was achieved and the evolution of an active relationship between New Zealanders and the beach is the story of changes in social attitudes to exercise, to leisure, to socialising between men and women and in public standards of 'decency'. Swimming in the sea allowed new freedoms of dress and behaviour which contrasted with the conventions of daily life and only furthered the popularity of the beach in the following years.

By the end of the 1920s, going to the beach was established as a popular recreation for New Zealanders. The following decades were to see that reputation consolidated and the flowering of a beach culture.

The beach expresses a number of fundamental things not available to the majority of us in our comparatively complex routines of urban life: at the beach — on holiday or just for the day — life is a great deal simpler. The environment and the summer heat allow a freedom in behaviour that would seem unusual at least at other times and places. There's the abandonment of unnecessary clothes, and there's the less inhibited social interaction that can be seen as mirroring the openness and freedom of the beach. Indeed romance has always been one of the chief occupations of the seaside holiday, one that is fostered by the informality of the surroundings. In the late nineteenth century, the beach was a place where young women could, without censure, let down their hair for the admiration of young men.

In the years since those first tentative dips in the briny, the beach has become an integral part of New Zealand life, the summer break 'at the beach' still regarded by many as the end-of-year prize for being a New Zealander. We grow up with rich, ingrained (like the sand of the beaches on which they were formed), ozone-charged memories of summer at the beach, which we treasure and add to throughout our lives: hair stiff with salt from a day in the waves, sand between the sheets, their white a coolness against heated skin, the smell of the sea, a full harvest moon rising out of the ocean, brown-as-berry limbs, winding, dusty metalled roads, ice blocks and ice cream, the crimson of pohutukawa, our native Christmas tree, collecting shellfish, poking around in rockpools, diving through the breakers. Being at the beach.

Taking *the* PLUNGE

Taking the Plunge

FOR MOST of the latter half of the nineteenth century, a visit to the beach was not the pastime of swimming and sunbathing of later decades. Rather, going to the beach on warm summer days was to picnic or to promenade. Children might paddle, but adults for their part remained clothed and dry, not to mention hot!

The popularity of swimming in the sea and the cult of the beach had its beginnings in the 1880s when the seaside, which up until then had been largely ignored as a place of recreation, first became fashionable. In England, in many of the countries of Europe and in the United States, 'sea-bathing' had long before been taken up as a desirable, health-promoting leisure pursuit, and it was a trend that now took root in Australia and New Zealand.

Going down to the sea to bathe owes much to a movement in Britain during the latter part of the 1700s that advocated sea-bathing as a cure-all. Among its promoters was one Dr Richard Russell who had published a paper outlining what he saw as the health-giving properties of seawater 'applied both externally and internally'.

Coinciding as it did with an increased public awareness of the need for hygiene and of the beneficial effects of the sun and exercise, sea-bathing provided an ideal combination of both hygiene and a moderate form of exercise. As well, of course, swimming in the sea was an inexpensive pleasure, free to all.

British bathing resorts of the mid eighteenth century gave impetus to the popularisation of sea-bathing and subsequently the whole beach ritual. By 1800, holidaying at the seaside in Britain had become fashionable. For workers of England's overcrowded cities and their families, a holiday at the seaside must have seemed about as far removed from their usual environment as it was possible to get.

In the absence of specifically-made bathing costumes, much of the bathing was done naked or in concoctions of undergarments, the men and women segregated on different parts of the beaches. For many women of the time, the bathing machine was a must. An English innovation from around the middle of the eighteenth century, the bathing machine was essentially a wheeled hut with doors at either end. Bathers changed into their costumes — if any — inside the machine and then later back into their dress clothes.

It's use permitted early swimmers to enter the water without a great need of specialised clothing, or any clothing at all. While some women wore undergarments into the sea, others were disinclined to expose the often delicate fabrics and lace to seawater, and so swam naked. Such women were commonly protected from the possibility of prying eyes by a cloak, fastened around the neck, which floated up shielding their torsos as they entered the water.

Towed out into the water by horses, the bathing machine was then turned around in a depth which allowed the bather to descend from the doors of the hut down a short ladder into the sea.

A further addition to the bathing machine, the 'modesty tunnel' was an awning which stretched over the sea-end door and shielded women entering the water until they were actually in the sea. In addition, the awning allowed even more private bathing beneath its covers, protecting the woman from public view, and the sun: a fashionable woman of the period was greatly concerned to maintain her pale complexion.

A longtime fixture on British and European beaches, the bathing machine made only a brief appearance in New Zealand; the idea never really caught on.

St Clair beach, 1880: lots of paddling but no one in swimming.

Bathing huts at Cave Rock Beach, Sumner, Christchurch, 1890s.

Redundant bathing machines, Caroline Bay, Timaru: aquatic modesty overtaken by pragmatism.

By the 1870s the absurdity of bathing machines was being questioned: 'the use of a man, a horse and a great house on wheels all to enable a human to dip himself in the sea!' While commonplace on European and British beaches for a number of decades, the duration of bathing machines on New Zealand's shores was brief, due in part, no doubt, to our lesser concern for what have been called the 'rituals of modesty'.

The explosion of interest in leisure-time sporting pursuits in the latter half of the century gave impetus to swimming, but in the beginning at least, this meant swimming in public pools, not at the beach. One of the country's oldest baths — and one still in use — is the St Clair Salt Water Baths that has been providing recreation for Dunedinites for 110 years.

In January 1884 the Caversham Borough Council (which encompassed St Clair) had written to the Dunedin City Council asking for funds to help extend and improve the baths which it had recently constructed by excavating a basin in the rocks at St Clair. The Caversham Borough Council pointed out the advantages of the site; it was well supplied with purest sea water, there was no danger from sea currents and it was accessible to the citizens of Dunedin and surrounding boroughs by tramcar. The question of public baths had long vexed the Dunedin City Council; older baths at the end of the old Pelichet Bay Jetty had become a health hazard, and finding a suitable site for new baths on the polluted edges of the harbour was difficult.

The Caversham Borough Council had timed its proposal well and the City Council decided after some investigations to grant a subsidy of £300 to the Borough, while also constructing its own baths at Logan's Point for a similar sum.

Both the Logan's Point and St Clair Baths were formally opened on 13 December 1884 and the newspaper report of the proceedings at St Clair makes interesting reading.

Before a crowd of some three hundred, 'a number of whom were ladies', the Mayor of Caversham, Mr Hugh Calder, made a short speech and then 'divested himself of his overcoat, and showed himself to be arrayed in Nature's garb, with the exception of a pair of bathing trunks, and without more ado took "a header" followed by about a dozen similarly attired persons'. The Mayor of Dunedin, Mr W. P. Street, arrived a little later, having just opened the Logan's Point Baths and, accompanied by Councillor D. M. Spedding, also indulged in a swim. The crowd was also entertained by the Industrial School Band. Later the swimmers and guests were treated to dinner in a nearby tent.

Swimming was for everyone, the perfect exercise, and one viewed by society as acceptable for the fairer sex. Indeed it became such a popular activity for women that one instructor of the period was encouraged to put pen to paper:

'Having taught swimming for the last three years, I may be considered competent to give a few instructions on paper. Very many people say "Oh, I'll never learn to swim, I'm too old", or "too stout", or "too thin", or "too weak", as the case might be, and so they never try. As a matter of fact everyone can learn to swim, old or young, strong or weak, stout or thin. It merely means a little more, or a little less time, according to the nerve and nature of the swimmer.

'The breast stroke is the most natural way to swim, and certainly the most graceful for a woman. It is the stroke the frogs use, and any one about to learn should catch a frog, put him into a tub, and study his actions when swimming, for

'Sketches at a Ladies' Swimming Contest', 1892. Swimming as exercise had begun to attract a large following, including many women. The consequent demand for swimming attire that allowed greater freedom of movement — as opposed to styles just to be seen in — encouraged the move to lighter-weight, more form-fitting costumes.

> SEA-BATHING
>
> If you are unaccustomed to sea-bathing, consult your doctor before you begin it.
>
> If you bathe in the early morning, take a biscuit and a little tea about an hour before your bath. Never bathe for at least an hour and a half after an ordinary meal.
>
> It is most important not to go into the water when very hot or very cold. A short walk before the bath, just sufficient to make you warm, and not hot, is the best. After your bath, a good walk will do you good.
>
> The whole body should be immersed at once if possible.
>
> Some people find it enough to get a good plunge or two and come out. Others can stay in ten minutes with impunity. Those who swim are often able to stay in longer than that. If in doubt, stay a short rather than a longer time.
>
> A smart rubbing with a rough towel is a very good thing after the bath.
>
> Dress quickly, without dawdling. If you can get a pail of hot water for your feet, as you often can do, it helps to promote circulation, and is a great luxury.

this is the action every swimmer has to imitate. The action with the arms is so simple that it really needs no teaching. My practice is always to show the pupil this arm stroke before taking her into the water at all, dividing it into three positions, first, second, and third. First, the arms close to the sides, hands extended, with the fingers close together, and the palms turned slightly out; second, the arms extended to the front, palms turned out; and third, the arms swept round in the stroke.

'When the pupil strikes out she should hold her fingers close together as if pushing her way through the water, and when she draws up her legs for the next kick she should straighten out the feet so that no resistance is offered to the water by the instep and in kicking out strike the soles of her feet, as it were against the water as if she was pushing herself up. The legs should be spread somewhat apart as she kicks, and when extended instead of drawing them up for a fresh kick she should draw them together closely. This is the best style for speed and can be acquired by any person who can swim in a very short time. A great deal depends on keeping time, the hands and feet moving together, or, to put it plainer, to kick the legs as the arms are being extended for the stroke and draw up the legs just as it (the stroke) is made. I have often thought that it would be much easier to teach swimming if good music was going on, for, like everything else it is best done to music.

'Bathing gowns should never be made of all cotton; flannel, flannelette, or any material composed of a proportion of wool are best. Serge I do not like, it being, when very good, too heavy, and when common too cold and too hard; and the best style for a bathing dress is the one that is the most easy to get off. For children the combination undergarment is very good, and for adults the short drawers, just reaching to the knee and buttoned round the waist with a wide band. Running strings are an abomination and most unhealthy. The breathing must on no account be interfered with in any way. The jacket should be as short as possible, just reaching a few inches below the waist, and without any sleeves. The lighter the dress is the better, have no frills or pleating about it, no trimmings or ornaments, nothing in fact, that can add to your weight or impede your course through the water.

'Many pupils come to me in expensive fashionable bathing gowns, very pretty to look at, but quite out of place while swimming. There are very nice jersey suits sold, made of half wool half cotton, they are excellent for swimming; but I would warn would-be purchasers to get them large enough — the commoner kinds (those containing most cotton) shrink very much, consequently they become too small after a few times wearing. I have a very vivid recollection of having to cut one of my pupils out of her bathing dress before she could even walk to her room from the bath, it having shrunk on her to such an extent that she could not move her limbs. So be warned and do not sacrifice comfort to a good fit.'

Swimming at the beach, however, was another matter altogether.

Bathing in the sea would become increasingly

popular during the 1890s — a popularity encouraged by the expansion of public transport to the 'marine suburbs' of New Zealand's towns and cities — but at the beginning of the decade public opinion was deeply concerned about the growing enthusiasm for New Zealanders to abandon the beach promenade for a dip in the briny and sought to discourage the tendency. In 1891 the Devonport (Auckland) Borough Council declared itself as definitely 'not in favour' of swimming by women or girls, and even limited the hours that males could bathe on the beaches within its jurisdiction — that they could do so only before 8 am and after 6 pm. Mixed bathing was forbidden.

It was a losing battle, however. Not only was the council unable to enforce any swimming curfew — indeed some visitors to the area's beaches provoked consternation by persisting in swimming during church hours on Sundays — but also found it impossible to compel male swimmers to use the accepted form of bathing costume or, in fact, any bathing suit at all. By 1893 the New Zealand Herald would report that:

'The bathing nuisance along the beach at the North Shore is once more becoming apparent.

'At the meeting of the Devonport Borough Council last night, several of the members spoke very strongly of the disgraceful behaviour of some of the bathers.

'At five o'clock last evening several young men were bathing in full view of the passers-by, in a perfectly nude condition.

'If complaints continue, bathing will probably be completely prohibited, thus inflicting a grievance on innocent persons through no fault of their own.'

The New Zealand Graphic in 1901 argued strongly for the liberation of the beach, in particular for legalising mixed bathing which, the magazine believed, would give impetus to the popularity of sea bathing, so that:

'One of the most delightful and healthful of summer recreations — and one to which our climate and unrivalled opportunities invite us — would become ten times more

A bucket and spade are useful, but for children even an old piece of timber will do at the beach.

Takapuna Beach, Auckland, 1890s: 'casting longing glances at the cool blue sea'. The times obliged adults at least to swelter through all the hottest days of summer. Children, on the other hand, might be allowed to remove their shoes and socks and to paddle in the cooling waves.

popular than it is. As it is now, we swelter through the dog days, and cast longing glances at the cool blue sea, but how comparatively few of us know the luxury of a noon-day dip. Yet there is every reason why such a thing should be as common as our noon-day meal.

'What makes the success of a picnic, the water party, the dance, but the co-mingling of men and women? A purely male or female picnic is a wearisome thing, and if Mrs Grundy were to insist on that division of men and women on the land . . . picnics would speedily cease to exist.'

The *Graphic* continued by highlighting the absurdity of segregating swimmers:

'Why that graceful form of garment should induce any particular shyness between man and woman is more than any one who regards the question rationally can conceive. Could we manage to get rid of the silly feeling, something like a social revolution would be the result. An enormous impetus would be given to sea-bathing, which would become the commonest, as it is the cheapest and most delightful, of all summer recreations.

'The sea would become the great rendezvous, as it is in America. It would be the most natural thing in the world to ask your lady friend to come in for a swim, as you might now invite her to come to afternoon tea at a tea-room. . . . The romantic possibilities of the thing, too, are not to be ignored. If friendships were fostered on Neptune's bosom, shall love among the breakers be denied?'

If the constraints imposed by officialdom were not enough, the would-be sea-bather also faced a poten-

A cartoon in the *New Zealand Free Lance Christmas Annual* of 1912 comments on the pleasant distractions in store for Wellington's city fathers when mixed bathing became a reality.

Dressing for the sea, Plimmerton, about 1910.

tially greater hazard in the form of sharks. These animals were then far more common close inshore and their presence posed a considerable threat to swimmers, one that was noted by commentators of the times. Writing about Auckland's North Shore, E. W. Payton described the area as having '... one or two long stretches of beautifully sandy shore ... but these cannot unfortunately be used much for bathing as the water is infested with sharks ... '.

Newspaper reports of other Auckland shark attacks from the period make chilling reading. One of the most striking harbour tragedies occurred off Wynyard Pier, Official Bay: 'A soldier was bathing there, when warning was given that a big shark was in sight. The bather, however, signified that he was not afraid, and was just boasting of the indignities he was prepared to inflict upon the shark when he was attacked and summarily bitten in two. Only enough of his body was recovered to make an excuse for a funeral.'

Another very poignant occurrence recalled by a Mr Robertshaw relates to St George Bay: 'The rock at the point sloped into the water in natural terraces, forming a popular bathing place. Two brothers named Bradley were swimming in the bay one day, and one of them, in coming out of the water, stepped upon a ground shark, which was basking on one of the terraces, in about 4 foot of water. The brute turned on him, and inflicted such terrible injuries that poor

AN UNUSUAL VISITOR: A SWORDFISH, CAUGHT RECENTLY IN HOBSON BAY, AUCKLAND.

One of the hazards of going for a dip in the early days: a report from 1904.

Bradley bled to death on the beach before assistance could be brought.'

Yet another case was that of a Mr H. Cooke, a well-known upholsterer, who was bathing from a rock at the foot of Hobson Street: 'As he was coming ashore a huge shark followed him and seized him by the leg. Cooke managed to free himself, but the shark persisted in its attack, and grabbed the leg again. After a desperate fight Cooke made good his escape, but with such injuries that his leg had to be amputated.'

It wasn't just the beach the authorities were concerned about. As the following report in a February 1892 issue of the *New Zealand Herald* makes clear, you weren't even safe out in the harbour:

'*Yesterday afternoon four men of the S.S.* Ruapehu *were taking a dip in the briny off the Railway Wharf, when they were observed by Constable Macky of the water police, who went in pursuit of them in a dinghy.*

'*On getting to them he found the men were all dressed in some sort of clothes as shirt and drawers. He got two of them to return to the steamer.*

'*It appears that the seamen were in ignorance of infringing any by-law, and it is conjectured that they were induced to take a bathe in the open sea from the fact that a seaman belonging to the S.S.* Dingadee, *in a spirit of bravado, said he would swim round the English steam-yacht* White Heather, *lying in the stream, and he was as good as his word.*'

For those members of Victorian society upset at the prospect of the public exhibition of the female form (though the first swimsuits tended to be more obscuring than revealing) agitation for mixed bathing represented an even greater moral outrage. In retrospect it is hard to imagine that the thought of mixed bathing should cause such consternation and horror, but one has to remember that we are talking of the same generation that could view a bare ankle or woman's calf as 'something shocking'.

However, the push for the liberation of mixed bathing saw officialdom and 'convention' losing out to a swelling tide of popular opinion. On the one side, 'society' which argued that immodestly-attired men and women mixing together in the surf would lead to a loosening of public morals, and, on the other, beachgoers who argued that it was only natural that the sexes should mingle in the sea as elsewhere. (Though, naturally enough, swimming and the beach were to allow greater possibilities for flirtation than were available in many other areas of Victorian life.)

By 1910, mixed bathing was a reality on most of the country's beaches, much to the delight of *Triad* magazine: 'Mixed bathing under decent conditions is a good thing for any community. It brings men and women back to a healthy human basis, and is an excellent antidote for the folly of peering prudes. When the sexes meet for a water-romp, all the nastiness of sexual pruriency is subdued and cleaned away. There is no evil suggestion in bathing-dress. And the bathing itself is a fine and wholesome tonic.'

With this achieved, the evolution of a bathing costume in which swimming could be truly enjoyed was inevitable. Even though, as before, it was an inevitability that society, as expressed by its laws, would be slow to accept.

For those who really wanted to swim, as opposed to splashing about in the waves, bathing costumes of the time were unwieldy and heavy, not to mention unflattering. But the protectors of the public morals were unyielding.

A New Zealand bathing belle of 1910.

'A Summer Seascape': a postcard from around 1910 depicting Ocean Beach, Dunedin. The expansion of electric tramways in the 1910s and 1920s gave impetus to the growth of seaside areas such as Christchurch's and Dunedin's ocean beaches.

'Mixed surf bathing', St Kilda beach, Dunedin, 1911. The bathers display a wide variety of costume styles, including small boys in shorts only and men in two-piece suits (one with hooped stripes), and women in sailor suit styles and two-piece woollen suits, their hair covered by oilskin caps. Opposition to mixed bathing existed through to the beginning of the twentieth century. In a radio broadcast of the 1950s, a Dunedin woman described her first encounter with mixed bathing. She recalled that as an eighteen-year-old in 1899, she had attended a beach cottage party where she was 'shocked to the marrow' to find men and women bathing together. She confided that she could never tell her parents that she had bathed in the breakers within shouting distance of a man.

Dressing for the sea, 1920s.

In its 1908 by-laws, Wellington City declared that: 'No person over the age of 10 years shall bathe on any beach within the view of any person or persons passing along any of the streets, thoroughfares, roads or public places of the City, or within the view of persons in any dwelling house in the City, unless such person so bathing shall be properly clad in a bathing garment reaching from the shoulder to the knee'.

In a 1912 addition to those regulations, parts of local beaches were declared for use solely by men or women. And in 1914: 'No male person in swimming costume who is over the age of 10 years shall be or remain on any beach foreshore open to the public . . . unless such person shall be clad in the swimming costume known as the Canadian Costume, or in a woollen neck to knee costume provided V shape trunks are worn underneath'.

The situation in other parts of the country was similar. A Napier Council by-law passed in 1894 had prescribed that: 'Provided nevertheless that every person bathing in the sea or in any river or other waters within, or within one mile of the boundaries of the borough of Napier, shall be attired in a decent and proper bathing dress, extending from the shoulders to six inches above the knees, no flesh coloured or net work dress to be considered decent and proper. Provided also that every person about to bathe, or who has bathed, as aforesaid, shall undress and dress in a bathing-machine, tent, or building, so constructed as to effectually conceal such person from view during the process of undressing.'

Dunedin city's 1898 regulations held that 'no person, over 10 years of age' shall be permitted to bathe except in proper bathing costume'. By 1916, this costume was being described in the Dunedin Ocean Beach Domain Board Act as:

'IN THE CASE OF MALES: In a bathing costume reaching from neck to knee with trunks or slips worn either inside or outside thereof.

'IN THE CASE OF FEMALES: In a loosely fitting bathing costume consisting of two garments and reaching from neck to knee.

'Provided that any person wearing the bathing costume known as the Canadian Costume shall be deemed to comply with this section; provided further that nothing in this section shall apply to any other child under the age of ten years.'

But if the beachgoers thought that that was the only restriction on their enjoyment of the sea and sand they were to be disappointed. You could go to the beach and, if you had the right togs, you could swim, but you couldn't loll about sunbathing:

'No person shall while attired in a bathing costume remain on the open beach except in the sea for an unnecessary space of time whether before or after bathing unless he also wears over such costume an overcoat or other garment effectually cloaking himself from neck to knee, provided that this section shall not apply to any person while endeavouring to save life or to any member of a life saving club engaged in life saving exercises and provided further that nothing in this section shall be deemed to prevent any person attired in bathing costume from remaining for the purpose of sun bathing or for physical exercise for any space of time in any part of the beach set apart by the Board for the purpose.'

For nearly as long as there have been New Zealanders swimming in the surf, there has been surf life-saving. As swimming in the sea became increasingly popular through the 1900s it was unavoidable that some swimmers should find themselves in trouble with rips and holes on boisterous surf beaches. The response was the formation — in 1910 — of the country's first surf life-saving clubs, at New Brighton beach, Christchurch, and Lyall Bay, Wellington. These were followed soon after by clubs at Castlecliff (Wanganui) and elsewhere.

The clubs were organised along the lines of the Australian surf clubs, the first of which, the Bondi Surf Bathers Life-Saving Club, was formed in 1906. Its founders were three Bondi surf swimmers who had developed the idea of a rescue line wound on to a portable reel that could be taken quickly to any part of the beach where it was needed in an emergency.

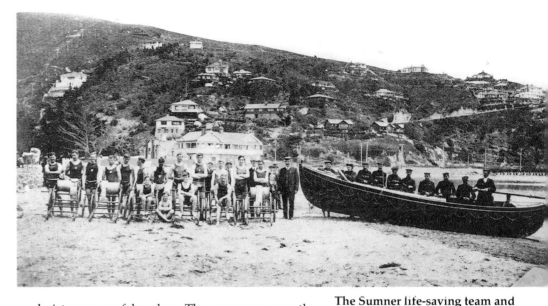

The Sumner life-saving team and their boat, *Rescue*, pictured at Clifton Bay about 1911.

RESCUES FROM SURF.

BATHERS AT LYALL BAY.

THREE BROUGHT ASHORE.

In spite of the fact that it was only the previous Sunday that several sensational rescues from the sea were made at Lyall Bay, three more bathers on January 5 disregarded the warning notices, with the result that they soon found themselves in difficulties in the strong undertow. It was only after strenuous efforts by Maranui and Lyall Bay life-savers that rescues were effected in each case.

The first exciting incident occurred about 3 o'clock in the afternoon, when a visitor from Masterton, a man, was caught in the dangerous undertow and carried out to sea. Fortunately his frantic efforts to save himself were observed in time by somebody on the beach and the matter was immediately brought to the notice of members of the Maranui and Lyall Bay Surf Clubs, who were in the tower of the clubs' shed.

Mr. E. Pocock, of the Lyall Bay Club, and Mr. F. Sleeman, of the Maranui Club, dashed to the assistance of the distressed bather, and after a hard struggle in the breakers succeeded in bringing him ashore. He was in an exhausted condition. After resuscitation methods had been applied he was able to proceed to his home.

At about 4.20 p.m. there was again excitement on the beach when it became known that some more bathers had got into difficulties in almost the same place. This time it was two young women, who were in danger of their lives. Messrs. Rankin and Sleeman, of the Maranui Surf Club, and Messrs. Dickson and Holland, of the Lyall Bay Club, went out to their assistance, while Messrs. J. Williams and A. Holland, also of the Lyall Bay Club, took out the reel and extra belts.

When brought to the shore, both women were very much exhausted, but after receiving attention were able to proceed to their homes. A man who was accompanying them was so pleased with the heroism shown by the Maranui and Lyall Bay life-savers that he at once made an appreciable donation towards the clubs' funds.

A club member stated subsequently that the whole trouble was again entirely due to the bathers disregarding the danger signals which had been placed at various places on the beach for their benefit. He added that the caretaker was constantly warning offenders, and that it was hoped that in future the practice of venturing out beyond the breakers would be discontinued.

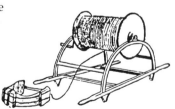

1932 saw the formation of the New Zealand Surf Life-Saving Association under which some 50 clubs from around the country were joined. Annual surf carnivals and championships ensure that life-savers maintain a high level of fitness and preparedness, qualities which have given them an international reputation. Preserved to the present day is the voluntary, humane spirit in which the service was formed, another reason why the work of the country's life-savers continues to be held in high regard.

Pleasures of the PICNIC

Pleasures of the Picnic

WELL BEFORE a visit to the beach had as its prime aim a dip in the briny, beachgoing had as its purpose the promenade or picnic. The latter has long been a national institution, its origins in the bush picnic of the first decades of European settlement, and achieved its greatest expression in the massed annual picnics that were major social events in the lives of New Zealanders in the nineteenth century and in the early years of the twentieth.

These picnics, most usually company, trade union, church or sporting club based, were frequently huge affairs, often complete with a printed programme of the day's events — detailing the menu to be enjoyed and competitions to be entered — beer by the barrel, and music. The public holidays from October through April eventually became a calendar of picnic days.

In the mid 1890s, the concerned picnic organiser could find in *An Antipodean Reference Book* suggestions for the successful picnic:

A picnic outing to Waihi Beach in the 1880s.

'HINTS ABOUT PICNICS

'It is better to take too much than too little.

'Pack sandwiches in a dry table napkin with a damp one rolled around the outside. And always cut them the last thing. If cut overnight they will be dry and stale by the luncheon hour. Salad is a favourite dish at picnics. Make the dressing before starting and carry it in a bottle. Cut the lettuce up just before luncheon.

'A plum pudding in which a number of coins, ring, thimble and button have been put makes much fun.

'Never take china plates, if you can avoid it, to a picnic. Proper paper plates made for the purpose are very cheap and easily obtained.

'Pressed tongues, round of beef, and hard-boiled eggs all make very nice sandwiches. Sardine sandwiches are also very good.

'When providing for a large number allow so much for each guest and a little over.

'Blanc manges, fruit pies, jellies, and all such soft things should be avoided as unsuitable for a picnic.

'If poultry is taken let it be carved before hand.

'If the tea has to be made in a billy, put the desired quantity of tea into a muslin bag before putting it into the boiling water.'

While our antipodean Christmas climate is at odds with that of the northern hemisphere, generations of New Zealand women manfully continued, despite heat and humidity, to serve up a hot midday Christmas 'dinner'... often at considerable cost to the digestion of both cooks and diners. In the last 30 years or so, however, as New Zealanders travelled more and were exposed to a wider variety of foods, our Christmas holiday fare has gradually adapted to the reality of a summertime Christmas. Now, for many, Christmas 'dinner' is a picnic or barbeque at the beach, or will combine cold cuts of traditional ham, chicken and turkey with a variety of salads, and a dessert of old-fashioned plum pudding and mince pies served alongside pavlova, strawberries and ice cream. (Conversely, midwinter is now frequently celebrated with a hot, sit-down meal that incorporates much of the traditional Christmas cuisine.)

At other times the beach picnic will most likely include one or more of the dishes that characterise New Zealand 'alfresco': a bacon-and-egg pie perhaps, or a green salad topped with mayonnaise, or an ad hoc feed of pipis collected and cooked there and then.

A popular choice for the mayonnaise, despite the many and varied proprietary brands to be found on supermarket shelves, is one made up using condensed milk and vinegar. 'Sally Lunn' in a column in a January 1948 issue of the *Weekly News* offered her version as follows:

Condensed Milk Mayonnaise

yolk of 1 hard-boiled egg
1/2 teaspoon mustard
vinegar
condensed milk
1 dessertspoonful sugar

Mix to a smooth paste with a little vinegar, the sugar, mustard and egg yolk. When quite smooth and free from lumps, add alternately a little vinegar and a little sweetened condensed milk, stirring all the time, until you have sufficient for your needs. This is very nice.

Regatta Day at Onerahi, Whangarei. In the early years of the century, swimming was not the popular pastime it would later become. Beaches were for picnicking, promenading or, as here, to watch regatta days from, and not for swimming or for lying around in the sun.

CHRISTMAS DINNER IN THE OPEN AIR
Happy campers enjoying their meal at Mercury Bay, Auckland Province.

The changing face of Christmas 'dinner'. Poet Syd Ribbands, in a poem written in the twenties, declared that 'They don't understand it at Home, / In the hemisphere north of the Line, / How we eat our mince pies under sapphire blue skies, / And whisk off the flies as we dine . . . '

Present at thousands of New Zealand picnics from the '30s through the early '60s, before the thermos displaced its function, was the Thermette. A picnic kettle that guaranteed boiling water in a matter of minutes, the Thermette was the invention of New Zealander John Hart. The patent was issued in 1930 — in respect of an invention for the 'means of use in heating water and cooking operations' — and manufacturing commenced a year later, with Thermettes available in a blue, orange or green finish.

Step one in its operation was to stuff crumpled bits of paper down the funnel, and then to add small sticks and twigs, whatever was to hand (ice block sticks and wrappers were useful and the frequent byproduct of any car trip). A match struck under this fuel would soon have the Thermette raising a healthy head of steam, with the promise of a cup of tea soon after.

The Thermette was also known as a 'chip heater' and the 'Benghazi Boiler', the latter name by virtue of its use in desert theatres of the Second World War when New Zealand army units carried Thermettes as standard issue, as the means of a quick cuppa during a lull in the fighting. Indeed the Thermette can accurately be said to have left its mark on the desert: it was reported that 'enemy troops overtaking Allied positions would know where the Kiwis had been from the round scorch marks on the sand, left by the circular fireboxes at the base of the Thermette'.

Boiling up a brew using the trusty Thermette.

(John Hart invented and marketed many other labour-saving products as well, among them an implement comprising a metal disc set at the end of a long handle that was used by thousands of New Zealanders to trim lawn edges along paths.)

Long before anyone ever thought of lying about on New Zealand's beaches, sandy sections of the coast performed another — more practical—function. For early Polynesian and European settlers, many of the country's beaches served as roads.

New Zealand's first settlements were around the coast, for obvious reasons. The country could only be approached from the sea, and the Maori economy in particular depended on it. The local beach and estuary provided the main food source, and rivers leading away from the coast were the means of access to inland bush for timber, birds and other resources.

Transport around the coast — perhaps to exploit more distant fishing beds or harrass a neighbouring tribe — was by canoe or on foot. In the case of the latter, beaches could offer a speedy passage, although there were often cliffs and the tide to consider.

Approximately one half of the North Island's west coast once served as a main highway, from Kawhia south almost to present-day Wellington. This route took advantage of every piece of existing beach, and although it connected inland settlements in more thickly inhabited areas, it never strayed far from the coast.

The land south of Kawhia, between Mokau and Pukearuhe, was home to the Ngati-Tama tribe, and the coast played an important part in their history. In parts their 'main road' crossed a sandy beach which was impassable at high tide, running underneath 275-metre high sheer cliffs. At one point this old Maori track confronted a barrier of land jutting into the sea, known

Commonplace at beaches at the turn of the century were entertainments such as merry-go-rounds, donkey rides, and coconut shys, like the one pictured here at Sumner.

'In Trouble': Golden Bay, Nelson, 1912. New and better roads, combined with increasing car ownership, meant that parts of the coast, once too far away for a daytrip, were now within reach. Although sometimes the cars found it hard going.

The pleasures of the picnic, long a New Zealand institution.

as the Taniwha's lair. There was no choice but to take to the cliff face, its ascent being assisted with stakes and supplejack rope handholds. It is here that Whiti, a chief of the Ngati-Maniapoto, was killed while attempting a precipitous escape from the enemy.

There is little wonder that this part of the country was so eagerly fought over: the coastal land was very fertile, the sea swarmed with fish and had some of the best mussel reefs on the whole west coast.

North of Waitara the coastal landscape levels out, staying comparatively flat all the way to Paekakariki. And from Patea, south of Mt Egmont (Taranaki), most of the traditional Maori coastal route consisted of fine hard sands, ideal for foot traffic. Arduous though it may have been, this form of transport was a blessing in disguise. The prevailing westerly winds on this coast made travel by canoe dangerous, and consequently there was less chance of incursions from enemy tribes. By contrast, the more sheltered east coast was better for coastal canoing expeditions, and in the early 1800s local tribes there suffered raiding Nga-Puhi war parties down from the north.

Maori travellers venturing south from Tamaki (Auckland) paddled canoes across the Manukau then carried them overland to the mouth of the Waikato River. The route eventually led down the Wanganui River to the coast, and beaches provided the route further south. Early European travellers appear to have preferred the coastal option to this inland river system. Thus, in the 1850s, a trip south began with a cart ride to Onehunga on the northern shores of the Manukau, from where canoes made the 16-kilometre crossing to Orua on the south head of the harbour. This was followed by a 50-kilometre trek along sandy beaches to the mouth of the Waikato.

Thereafter the traveller stuck to the coast nearly all the way to Wellington, crossing rivers and scaling cliffs as required. It seems that only at New Plymouth was there anything resembling a formal route — a 16-kilometre section of cart road. Even so, it's hard to imagine it comparing in comfort to a hard sandy beach.

A seaside picnic.

The old metal bucket and wooden spade may have yielded to plastic equivalents in the present day but these two items remain essential beach accessories for the very young. A day out at Ngamotu Beach, New Plymouth.

The fully clothed beachgoer at the turn of the century could still partake in paddling, the essence of which has been described as, in fact, the 'feel of water on the bare legs of an otherwise clothed body'.

Although there are still pockets of isolated beach communities accessible only from around the coast at low tide, nowadays the most likely persons to travel any distance on sand are tourists to the Far North, bounding up the hard surface of Ninety Mile Beach.

Today's standard car-owning family enjoys more flexibility in their planning than did their early twentieth century counterparts travelling to the seaside by bus, tram or train, but trips to the beach still require preparation. Well prior to getting family and gear together, there's the weather and the tide to consider. With the car packed and the kids consigned to the back seat, the journey may entail some fairly dusty and winding roads: generally, the price of avoiding the crowds is a bit of travelling discomfort. However, once there, all is forgotten on the sand and in the surf . . . at least until the whole process is repeated in reverse. (Though by now the discomfort is increased by tiredness, sunburn and back-seat congestion. And the situation may not be helped by announcements concerning lost jandals, and the realisation that, for some, there may be homework still to be done for school next day.)

A family trip to the beach will also demand a boot full of equipment, covering all eventualities. Even the earliest toys available to New Zealand children reflected the country's proximity to the sea: wooden buckets and spades were available in local shops by 1845. By the 1920s, the buckets — or pails — were of metal, initially plain but soon in bright colours and designs. The essential accessory was the wooden spade, made in one piece with 'smooth, rounded edges', and four sizes. Better suited for excavating wet sand was the metal version, only 6d in 1936. By the early 1950s the spade had combined the best of both materials — metal base and a long wooden handle — while buckets decorated with nursery rhymes were recommended for making sandcastles.

Other early toys were less suited to the rigours of the New Zealand beach. Clockwork launches may have performed well in a placid tub or pond, but would have quickly floundered or rusted at the beach. A more satisfactory pursuit would have been a 10" diameter beach ball, of 'durable rubberized fabric and with pure gum balloon bladder' — just 3/11 in 1932.

By the 1950s, beach accessories — not just toys — were a booming business. It was this decade that saw the first appearance on our beaches of a footwear style that eventually came to be synonymous with the beach. This was the jandal (or 'thong' as the Aussies will have it), first sported in this part of the world by the Japanese swimming team at the 1956 Melbourne Olympics. The practical footwear caught the imagination and was soon being worn by New Zealanders in their thousands. With a name derived from 'Japanese sandal', the jandal was first manufactured in an Auckland garage.

Originally available only in a brown-and-white colour combination, plain colours and candy-striped jandals followed, with blue proving the most popular colour. Today the jandal has been largely superseded by the fashion for all-purpose trainer shoes, an upmarket derivative of the appropriately named 'sand-shoe'.

Aside from the ubiquitous jandal, whose wear was not restricted to the beach, the most popular item of the '50s and '60s was probably the lilo. This air mattress began life as a camping aid, providing welcome relief from sagging camp stretchers. It was also found to be buoyant in the sea, opening up new possibilities, but the largest of these rubber monsters — up to 76 inches (193 cm) long by 30 inches (76 cm) wide — could be both unmanageable and hazardous in the surf, and were best left for the adults. Beyond the breakers and at the mercy of wind and current they could carry unwary occupants out to sea.

In the lilo family there were also water wings, beach balls and rings, and a surfboard of 'firm, unsinkable rubber' with pointed bow and handgrips. Perhaps the biggest drawback with lilos was inflation. Although there were pumps for the job it was often a case of everyone having a puff. At the end of the day, if it hadn't deflated by itself, the lilo would have to be let down before it could be forced into the car boot.

Excursion steamers at the wharf, Days Bay, Wellington, in the 1920s. In the days of the mass picnic, steamers were a popular means of transport to coastal and island destinations. Eventually, improved roading and greater private mobility reduced the use of steamers to many of these destinations. The boat trip to Days Bay, however, continued to be popular long after this method of transport had been superseded, preferable as it was to the alternative of a lengthy journey around the harbour.

HOLIDAY JOYS

AIR BEDS

for fun anywhere under the sun

An alternative improvised inflatable gave as much fun as the official lilo version. An obese inflated black tractor inner tube made a hilariously slippery 'castle', to be defended against all intruders.

Recent additions to the catalogue of beach 'toys' include skimboards and the popular boogy board, both of which greatly increase the fun to be had at the beach.

Young New Zealanders are traditionally introduced to beaches with the assistance of buckets, spades and water-wings. Eventually, however, parental control is outgrown and young teenagers can enjoy a taste of freedom at the beach. Swimming is, to some extent, still on the programme, but now there are other diversions. Suntans need to be worked on, swimsuits compared, and always a watchful eye kept on the opposite sex. Gangs of callow youths gaze across the sandhills, their furtive interest being hardly discouraged by the girls. Inevitably, refreshments are needed, and trips made to the local shop, with the hope that convenient encounters might occur.

For a start, most of what goes on consists of observation, talk and idle fantasy. Groups parade up and down the beach, ostensibly to be seen, a modern version of the promenade. Eventually, when the objects of desire become accessible, the beaches can continue to accommodate the continuing relationships. Sandhills, with convenient clumps of vegetation placed some distance from the general crowd, are handy for such purposes. As, of course, is the car and a secluded parking site.

The rituals of the beach are both numerous and distinctive. Such is the freedom of the sand that many of its associated activities would not be tolerated elsewhere. Beachgoers can now, it seems, wear as little as they like, and few people complain if they do. The arrival of the bikini was a shock for some, but nowadays the top part is often dispensed with as well. Even so, the practice is not yet so commonplace as to go unnoticed, as is the case in the South of France. Topless

Eastern Beach, Auckland. One of the effects of ageing — similar to the process by which policemen appear younger each year — is that one declares past summers to have been warmer, sunnier, and longer than in recent times. In respect of the first, however, average temperatures over New Zealand have, in fact, increased since 1950 by about 0.5°C (which may or may not be the result of increased carbon dioxide in the atmosphere).

With a portable record-player, beachgoing teenagers of the mid sixties could spin their favourite 45's while enjoying the summer sunshine.

sunbathing in New Zealand is still guaranteed to encourage a degree of gregarious behaviour in some males, an impromptu and highly unseasonable game of touch rugby being a typical response. The aim of the game is not so much to score — with the ball, that is — but to impress the 'talent'. The peaceful ambience of the beach is therefore shattered by a bunch of sweaty jocks hurling themselves about on the sand. Fortunately, it doesn't usually last for long, and other beachgoers tend to doze on in the knowledge that such blatant displays are mostly ineffective.

Music beside the seaside probably began with band rotundas, once standard features at city beaches. It was not until the 1950s that beachgoers could take — or make — their own summer sounds, though these were inevitably English or American. With the arrival of portable record players they could spin such discs at the beach as Nat King Cole's anthem to everlasting fun in the sun, 'Roll out those lazy, hazy, crazy days of summer. . .'. (This may have fitted the mood of the times, but this song hardly reflected New Zealand conditions, with mention of 'soda and pretzels and beer'. The first went under another name here, the second was unheard of, and it was illegal to consume the latter in a public place — particularly if under age.)

Perhaps the artist who best set the mood for music at the beach in the late 1950s was Harry Belafonte, his classic 'Banana Boat Song' and 'Island in the Sun' (both 1957) reflecting the current vogue for things Caribbean. Three years later there was a less serious tribute to changing fashions at the beach, in Brian Hyland's 'Itsy Bitsy Teeny Weeny Yellow Polka Dot Bikini'.

The late 1950s was also the time of Burl Ives' 'Pearly Shells' and Pat Boone's 'Love Letters in the Sand'. Another American perspective on romance at the beach was provided in the early sixties by the Drifters; their 'Under the Boardwalk (. . . down by the sea . . .)' became part of every aspiring rock group's repertoire.

The 'surf sound' of the sixties was led by Californians: the Beach Boys (who couldn't actually surf) and Jan and Dean (who could at least ride skateboards). Their songs were less about riding the waves and

more about a mythical lifestyle that promised 'Fun, Fun, Fun' and 'Two Girls For Every Boy'. And no respectable dance band in those days could get away without a version of the manic instrumental 'Wipe Out', made famous by the Surfaris in 1963.

Strange as it may seem, New Zealand's coastline is equal in length to that of the United States. No doubt this has a lot to do with our country consisting of islands with extremely ragged edges. Also, our general north-south orientation ensures a wide range of conditions for beachgoers. All of this is particularly good news for surfriding, a sport which arrived here in the 1920s from Hawaii. It was to provide a further use for our beaches, and new purpose to many of our coastal towns.

In its earliest days, surfriding was associated with surf life-saving. It developed its separate identity and modern image in Hawaii and California in the mid 1950s, reaching New Zealand in 1959 after demonstrations by two visiting American surfers at Piha and Oakura (Taranaki). The idea quickly caught on, and in 1962 New Zealand became the first country in the world to have a national organisation for the sport. By then the country also had its first two surfriding clubs — Auckland's North Reef Club and The Point Boardriders Club of Hamilton.

By the end of the decade there was a sizeable subculture of surfers, or 'surfies' as they were then known. The New Zealand Surfboard Riders Association claimed 9000 members, and there were plenty of others too busy riding the waves to register. Four factories in Auckland alone were knocking out boards, and one store claimed to have sold 300 during the summer of 1968. A cult was born: the pursuit of the perfect wave, Kombie vans and old stationwagons, sleeping on the beach, a diet of hamburgers, eggs and chips, Buzz Bars and milkshakes, and a whole subculture of music (the Beach Boys), clothes (baggies), films (including local variants such as *Out of the Blue* and *Endless Summer* by New Zealand surfing movie pioneer Tim Murdoch), and a language all of its own, replete with 'hanging five' and 'lefthanders'. Summer weekends would see carloads of youths driving hundreds of miles — often criss-crossing the country — in their search for the perfect wave, waxing their boards, and adding to the surfing knobs below their knees.

In the early days of surfing — before neoprene wetsuits — football jerseys were part of the New Zealand uniform, complementing longish shorts, or 'baggies', white zinc ointment and bleached hair. The presence of surfers — most usually distant figures bobbing beyond the breakers, patiently waiting for the next big one — gradually became part of the scene.

The influence of the sport spread far beyond the beaches, reaching even our radios and footpaths.

Words such as 'ding' and 'wipeout' entered the language. A dry land spin-off was skateboarding, a sport that has since become a mode of transport. In the '60s it was taken up by teenagers on homemade boards with steel wheels recycled from their own childhood skates. A generation later it, too, has a subculture of its own, with distinctive music, clothing and intrepid acrobatics.

At first, the surf boards used were veritable monsters, 16 feet (4.9 metres) long and of solid wood. Later they were reduced to 14 feet (4.25 metres) using hollow plywood construction. In the early sixties the modern plastic process was born, but at 10 feet (3.0 metres) these new boards, although lighter, were still lengthy affairs, and still could be carried only on car roofracks or in the backs of stationwagons. In recent years boards — now polyurethane foam and fibreglass combinations — have shrunk considerably, and can be squeezed (with a bit hanging out the window) into the average car.

With more than 300 separate 'spots', this country can claim some of the finest surfing beaches in the world. Every surfer has a favourite haunt and Raglan is favoured by many. There is only the prevailing westerly wind and 2000 kilometres of Tasman Sea between it and Australia. Southwest of the township, at the northern foot of Karioi Mountain, is Whale Bay and 'The Point', the scene of New Zealand's most famous surf break. Here, 3.5-metre breakers regularly

Boardsurfing in the 1920s made use of shortish wooden boards. The Duke of Gloucester, seen here heading into the breakers at Piha beach in Auckland, was introduced to the sport while in New Zealand on a visit in 1934.

provide one-kilometre long rides for confident surfers. To add to its allure, this rocky cove has no beach to speak of: its boulders can demolish loose boards.

A good surfing wave is the result of particular swells and wave-breaks. The two different types of swells are ground and wind swells. The source of the former is thought to be a combination of currents, tides and storms, while the cause of the other is obvious. New Zealand's west coast has no shortage of wind swells, lying as it does in the face of the prevailing westerly, and the east coast is noted for ground swells supplied by the Pacific.

Having identified the swells, there are then four basic types of waves, or breaks, encountered around New Zealand. The most common is the beach break, where the action of the sea is influenced by the shifting sands on its bottom. When this consists of a long gentle slope the resulting wave may be ideal for novice surfers, and perhaps essential training for the point break. This occurs when the swell moves parallel to a headland, and usually demands a rocky bottom. The result can be the 'ideal' wave, and the most reliable source of these is Raglan.

Distinctive waves are also caused when swells break over submerged material such as rocks and reefs. Taranaki is particularly acquainted with this variety, the action of the swells hitting lava reefs from the province's extinct volcano being capable of producing waves in excess of 7.5 metres. And finally, the fourth type of wave is that produced at the mouth of a river. Although similar to the beach break, this surf can be complicated by currents and rips.

The black ironsand beaches of Auckland's Muriwai, Maori Bay, Bethells and Piha all offer scope for northern surfers. Aucklanders who don't wish to drive over the Waitakere Ranges can try more gentle conditions at Milford or Takapuna, or further north on the Shore, at Orewa or Red Beach. Out in the Gulf, various points at the eastern end of Waiheke Island promise suitable surf during a large swell, and Awana, Medlands and Kaitohe Beaches on Great Barrier Island work best at high tide.

South of Auckland and over the Coromandel Peninsula is the ever popular surf beach of Whangamata with its estuary, beach and bar, and Whitianga and spots around Waihi. Elsewhere on the North Island's West Coast are Waikato Heads, Castlecliff (at the mouth of the Wanganui River), and the various possibilities of Cape Egmont. Due to the shape of the latter it is possible to select beaches according to the wind.

The appropriately named Bay of Plenty and East Coast also offer a plenitude of surfing opportunities. Eastwards from Mt Maunganui (otherwise known as The Mount) is a succession of beaches: Omanu, Matata, Ohope and Opotiki. Then, around the East Cape lie the Mahia Peninsula and Gisborne and the long sandy stretches of Waikanae (which boasts a 'pipeline'), Wainui and Makorori. The former beach has claimed the country's most consistent surf, while the area regularly hosts the national boardriding championships.

Further south in Wellington, the capital offers scope for surfing at Eastbourne, and at Island, Houghton and Lyall Bays — the latter noted for its 4.5-metre right reef break. But for North Island surfers who can't make it to the coast, Lake Taupo may be the answer. Te Pokei Point on its eastern shore offers a small left point break . . . but only during a strong southerly.

South Island surfers are generally restricted to Nelson, Marlborough and the east coast, many of the West Coast beaches being steep, gravelly and exposed to ferocious westerly weather. St Clair and St Kilda near Dunedin are known for their surf, as are New Brighton, Sumner and Scarborough beaches in Christchurch.

One of the most popular pastimes around the coast of New Zealand is beachcombing — exploring and foraging for flotsam and jetsam. The sea is full of surprises and at times deposits some of these on our beaches.

Coastal residents are particularly well placed for such foreign arrivals, but even daytrippers to the beach can encounter the occasional oddity. Such was the case in 1966 when three turtles and a sea snake were found on Ninety Mile Beach. The turtles — one a Hawksbill and another a Giant Green variety — were sent to the Napier Aquarium, but the snake was not so lucky. It was a venomous and therefore unwelcome arrival and was quickly disposed of with a piece of wood.

Turtles have arrived here frequently over the years, as have such items of Pacific vegetation as tropical beans, coconuts, palm trunks and fronds. Some of the beans have been successfully grown in gardens in Northland, and coconuts have been known to arrive here still edible.

Beachcombers may secretly dream of discovering washed-up chests of old pirate treasure, or perhaps a piece of eight or two, but probably the closest New Zealanders have got to this is ambergris. An ash-coloured waxy substance, derived from a biliary secretion of the spermaceti whale, ambergris was once regularly found on our west coast beaches. There are fewer whales now so it is less common, and synthetics have now superseded its use in the perfume industry. However, in 1967 it was reported that one fortunate beachcomber had sold a parcel of several pounds weight of the substance for 15/- an ounce (then about $53 per kilogram).

A rather different type of booty from the sea began appearing on New Zealand's beaches in the 1960s. They were Japanese fishing floats; spheres of blue, green as well as clear glass. These were eagerly sought after as decorative additions for the bach or home. With the added realism of a section or two of fishing net they were commonly used to effect a nautical look

Daytrippers at Mellons Bay in Auckland. A generous use of canvas provides shade for vehicles as well as people.

A summer's picnic in the shade of a pohutukawa.

in contemporary coffee bars and restaurants of the day. Such floats — which could also be Portuguese in origin — were worth about $20 each on the secondhand market in the early seventies.

The Japanese fishing industry fleet has inadvertently provided New Zealand with a lot more in the way of flotsam. Large blue saki bottles (some with labels intact), plastic rice bowls and chopsticks, plastic containers of all descriptions, wooden-soled deck sandals and bamboo rods have all come ashore here, especially on the west coast of Northland.

Many of these items are interesting enough souvenirs of a day at the beach, but some can be put to practical — as well as decorative — use. Japanese bamboo casks and barrels are exquisite examples of the cooper's art, there being no nails in their construction. When polished up and varnished they can convert into attractive firewood containers. Line markers have also been found, and to preserve some sort of international balance are often weighed down with a stone from a Japanese beach. They may still carry a tattered flag and have a plastic ball-float attached, while fish have often been found containing the distinctive Japanese hook, which is very similar in shape to that traditionally used by the Maori. Broken tuna rods, gaffs and self-draining longline boxes have also come ashore, the latter being slotted on four edges to accommodate up to 180 hooks and traces.

The romantically inclined beachcomber may also search for the elusive message in a bottle. Such items have been found, but most are of a fairly practical nature. In early 1970 an Auckland family with a holiday home at Glinks Gully, a coastal settlement south of Dargaville, regularly scoured the local beaches

Picnicking at Titahi Bay, Wellington, in the thirties.

HOLIDAY OUTINGS

HEAVY MOTOR TRAFFIC

CHANGE IN THE WEATHER

A boisterous westerly wind and heavy rain squalls at Auckland on Monday made conditions unpleasant for the observance of Christmas Day out-of-doors. Many of the most popular bathing beaches, which attract large crowds in fine weather, were sparsely patronised, and even the main roads did not carry the volume of holiday traffic that is customary at this time of the year. Numerous yachts and motor-launches took advantage of the long week-end to make cruises to favourable anchorages within sailing distance of Auckland, but the rough weather detracted considerably from the enjoyment of the outings.

On Saturday, motor traffic was reported by Automobile Association patrols to be the heaviest ever seen north of Auckland. The vehicular ferries ran a continuous service the whole day, and long lines of cars could be seen awaiting the arrival of each boat at Auckland. There was an endless stream of traffic along the roads to the north, and there were over 100 campers between Silverdale and Waiwera. Traffic was still proceeding north on Sunday, and cars also began to arrive in Auckland from the south. It is anticipated there will be large numbers of cars on the roads to-day, owing to the postponement of so many holiday journeys yesterday on account of the weather.

and found a number of sealed jars containing messages. As it turned out they had all been liberated from the nearby Kaipara Harbour. The Ministry of Works had been conducting drift tests to find a possible site for New Zealand's first nuclear power station!

Three of these jars were picked up within a kilometre or two of each other but the fourth must have taken advantage of some quirk of wind and current, ending up at the Maunganui Bluff, some 110 kilometres north. The same section of coastline has been privy to other messages in bottles: one in Spanish and another in what was presumed to be Arabic.

In the early 1980s many beaches in the Auckland area received a new and unwelcome foreign arrival in the form of small white plastic pellets. Their origin is something of a mystery, but they floated ashore and became intermixed with the sand. They may have been pellets from imports of plastic 'feedstock' for the local plastics industry that had been somehow released at sea, or some kind of packing material washed ashore from container ships, but another suggestion put the source closer at hand. They may have been an industrial by-product that had entered the stormwater system and found its way to the sea.

Nature itself ensures a regular supply of marine curiosities and casualties to our shores. The novice beachcomber might well be surprised — or repulsed — by a first encounter with goose barnacles, for example. These consist of shells (upwards of 4 cm long) at the end of 15- or 20-cm flexible leathery stalks. Much less unusual but decidedly more dangerous is the common jellyfish. The deflated bodies of these lilac-coloured animals are often found abandoned at high water mark around our beaches.

In addition there are always interesting shells — from bearded mussels to horse mussels (up to 45 cm long) and fragments of our opalescent paua, as well as geological specimens, bits of driftwood and skeletal remains of sea birds and fish.

Beachcombing is a healthy pursuit, guaranteeing fresh air and perhaps a few curios for the mantelpiece at home. But it can serve a further purpose — the surveillance and maintenance of our beaches. The proliferation of plastics and packaging materials has had an unfortunate effect on parts of our coast. It does nothing for our once natural environment and can be disastrous for the animals that frequent our beaches.

BEACH DAZE

('Thousands Throng Beaches' — Newspaper headline)

Come along, kiddies, and crack your whip, Mum,
All into the car, if you please.
To-day's just the day for a picnic, I'm sure —
Sing-ho for a bracing sea breeze!
For heaven's sake, Billy, you can't bring all that:
A bucket, three spades, two boats and the cat!

Don't worry so, Mum, the iron's turned off —
I should know, I pressed my own pants!
I'm watching the traffic, we've got enough lunch,
I don't drive as if in a trance.
What was that bang? Now then, Betty, Don't yell —
We've just had a blowout! Pile out, folks! Oh, well!

Ah, there is the beach, just look at that sea!
I'll race you all in for a swim.
Where are my togs, Jack? You left them behind?
I say, son, that's a bit grim!
Those life-saving fellows are quick on the job.
Wonder who's drowning? Good grief, it's our Bob!

Stop worrying, Mother, the iron's turned off —
Just fill up my tea and don't fret.
Please use a towel, Bill, we brought at least ten,
You're making my shirt sopping wet.
Sweet little Betty — I'll boil you in tar
For burying deep the keys of the car!

Never mind, kiddies, we're nearly back home —
We're sunburnt and tempers are short.
But why all the firemen around in our street?
Ye gods, that's just what I thought!
Look lovingly, children, that smouldering sight
Proves for all time that your Mother was right!

(— ARIEL, *The New Zealand Observer*, March 1952)

A summer's day, 1957. Even an only halfway decent day at the beach more than compensates for any of the drawbacks such as getting the tide wrong, sand in the sandwiches, a beach umbrella that didn't work, and returning home burnt, tired and short-tempered.

Going down to the sea is for many New Zealanders also a matter of messing about in boats or on windsurfers. Sailing is a skill that seems second nature to this country's inhabitants, not surprising given that the lives of most of us are so influenced by the sea.

Without a doubt the most famous of the country's yacht classes, the P class has a proud history in the best traditions of New Zealand do-it-yourselferism and enterprise.

Designed by Harry Highet and the first prototype built by him, the boat was conceived as a simple training yacht that 'any boy could build for himself using pine planking and simple tools: something that boys could build with a little help from their fathers'. And indeed the P class has proved to be 'the' design that young New Zealanders have grown up with and cut their sailing teeth on. Most name yachties can hark back to learning their trade through the idosyncrasies of P class sailing, including how to capsize and right the craft.

The class had its origins in a request to Harry Highet from a friend for a small yacht suitable for a beginner, preferably unsinkable but with a reasonable performance. At the time Harry Highet mostly built 14-footer yachts so his response was to make a halfsize version. And the P class is still built to 7 feet today.

Boating in the 1900s.

In 1922 Harry Highet moved to Tauranga where the P class was adopted and indeed became known for a time as the Tauranga Class. In 1924 it became officially the P class. Seventy years on it remains a popular learning and racing class, with the annual national champs sailed for the Tauranga Cup, and for the Tanner Cup.

Harry Highlet and Jim Gilpin, three-time winner of the Tauranga and Tanner Cups. (1951)

The experience of small boat sailing is at the root of New Zealand's leadership in international yachting competition. And to a large degree that experience is aboard a P class, or, as it was for a time, the T (for Tauranga) class.

Beauty and the BEACH

Beauty and the Beach

TODAY'S BEACH BY-LAWS simply regulate that beachgoers should be, at least, 'properly or sufficiently clad'. Indeed the relevant clause is so open to interpretation that most district councils would be reluctant to take action today against topless bathing or even fully nude bathing unless patently indecent or offensive. In the early years of the century, however, a proliferation of laws described in detail just what was — and what was not — allowed. Indeed such a regulation — requiring that swimmers at its beaches must wear a neck-to-knee style swimsuit — is still on the books in Wanganui.

When New Zealanders patronised city beaches in the 1880s it was to picnic and promenade, and not to exploit the sun or sea. For those few men and women who braved both the waves and the censure of society, swimming attire, in the absence of a specially designed costume, was often a cobbled together assemblage of undergarments. That is, when clothing was worn. Men in particular frequently swam naked.

The story of the evolution of the swimsuit at the New Zealand beach is one that has been determined by changing attitudes towards leisure, public standards of decency, and developments in clothing manufacture and technology. It had its beginnings in the mid 1880s when the increasing interest in leisure sports — such as cycling, tennis and golf — by an emerging middle class demanded new kinds of less formal attire. When it came to bathing suits, it would be necessary of course that these should still maintain the degree of modesty the times required. However, as will be seen, the beach soon came to be regarded as some kind of neutral ground where modesty would, of necessity, be temporarily suspended.

The first costumes — fussy, voluminous and fashioned neck-to-knee — worn by women bathers of the late nineteenth and early twentieth centuries were designed as much with showiness and fashion in mind as swimming. They gave way in the early 1910s to the more figure-fitting 'Canadian' costume which, while figure-clinging and heavy when wet, represented a huge step forward on the path to swimsuits that were comfortable to wear and which allowed real freedom of movement. For now men and women were wanting to go to the beach to swim and not just frolic in the waves. By the end of the 1920s, women's swimwear was more like men's, halter-topped and with the overlapping tunic skirt now much reduced or disappeared altogether, a transition to a one-piece suit that was buoyed along by the then current fashion for exercise and fitness, and the desire to expose as much of one's skin as seemly to the health-promoting rays of the sun. That desire — to reveal one's skin to the sun and to do so in an attractive way — continues to the present day to be the prime motivation behind both men's and women's swimsuit design.

The first women's swimsuits were of heavy, cloaking fabrics, fashioned neck-to-knee. In 1893, a fashion column in the New Zealand Graphic and Ladies' Journal indicated that 'the most modest and suitable' form of attire for women to bathe in was a neat jacket of serge with a band around the waist, and loose trousers or drawers ending with a frill just below the knee, with a skirt of the same fabric over the top.

The most usual colours for women's bathing dresses were navy and black. The fabric seersucker was also recommended because it 'blew out' from the body when it was wet and had the advantage of not

Advertisements from the 1908 Sears, Roebuck Catalogue show the similarity of women's bathing costumes to daywear of the time. And how impractical such costumes were for actual swimming.

Women beachgoers of the 1900s.

**This group of swimmers from 1910 wear trunks over their woollen suits which, when wet, were figure-hugging in the extreme. The trunks, usually V-shaped, were often a requirement of local by-laws.
Inset: Men's swimming costumes as advertised in the Sears, Roebuck Catalogue for 1908.**

being as absorbent as woollen materials. To produce just one of these garments it has been estimated that about thirty-three metres of fabric would have been required. These costumes were weighty and hampered the would-be swimmer well into the first decade of the twentieth century.

According to Marguerite, the fashion columnist for the *New Zealand Graphic and Ladies' Journal*, it was crucial that women's bathing costumes were made large and loose. She had recently observed a group of women preparing to bathe clad in dainty, tight-fitting, cotton princess garments. These women had subsequently emerged from the sea with their bathing costumes clinging limply to their figures 'revealing every curve' in a manner which apparently 'provoked some very uncomplimentary and stinging remarks from a few gentlemen who had gathered on the beach'.

Styled more for show, rather than for actual bathing, the cumbersome, heavy construction of these costumes meant that swimming was difficult anyway. Women were also hampered by society's view that vigorous exercise of any kind was not appropriate for the fashionable woman. That said, it was a view that could be expected to hold more sway in Britain, unlike New Zealand or Australia where less strongly held social conventions, and more equable climates, must have encouraged a more relaxed attitude to women's sports.

Men in the 1890s swam in 'long johns'-like bathing suits that covered them from midcalf to the elbow. Disconcertingly similar in appearance to underclothing of the period, such swimwear was usually made up in bold styling — with hooped stripes for instance — in an attempt to play down an association with undergarments. By the early 1900s, men's bathing suits had become sleeveless and had shortened to mid-thigh to give greater freedom of movement in the water. For modesty, briefs were commonly worn over men's bathing costumes, which, when wet, could leave little to the imagination.

With the legalising of mixed bathing in the 1910s, by-laws governed the style of swimwear that men and women could wear into the surf. So that Laidlaw Leeds, wholesale merchants in Auckland, offered in 1917 a ladies' 'two-garment bathing costume in the most approved style'. Of woven cotton in dark navy with stripes, this claimed to be 'very elastic', and would 'fit any figure'. A male costume of the same year was a sleeveless two-piece outfit 'now demanded by the authorities in most districts'. Available only in navy blue with white edging, this was similar to the ladies' model — particularly so when sagging from saltwater absorption.

Bathing caps 'to protect all the hair' were also available from Laidlaw Leeds for 1/6 each, and sun glasses with 'smoked blued panes' at *6d* per pair.

For women the advent of the 'Canadian' costume in the early 1910s was a blessing, a sensible design for swimmers which consisted of a pair of woollen knickers which reached half way to the knees, and a tunic also of wool which went over the knickers and hung to the middle of the thighs. It was a style that became standard wear for women for many years, until superseded by the one-piece swimsuit in the 1930s. And the Canadian suit was one that found favour with the authorities, now having to face up to mixed bathing on their beaches and concerned as ever that modesty should be maintained — especially now that women would be gambolling in the water alongside men.

By 1920 the Canadian swimsuit was being manufactured locally as the 'Colonial all-wool bathing costume', available in Maids', S.W., W. and O.S. sizes. Within three years the traditional navy colour was supplemented with facings of gold and saxe (slate or stone), with saxe-putty another combination. Also, rubber bathing caps with trimmings of rubber flowers or bows were now available, though photographs from the time indicate most women were happy to stay with the older, shower-cap style oilskin cap.

A happy group enjoying the waves despite their heavy, clinging, restricting costumes. Anyone who ever wore a woollen suit of the kind that was popular in the 1920s remembered the experience for the rest of their life: the encumbrance that was the wet woollen fabric, the chill of sodden serge and flannel that dried only slowly.

It was in the 1920s that the most dramatic advances were made in the development of a more utilitarian bathing costume for women. Styles in swimwear continued to follow the fashionable silhouette for outerwear, and so there evolved a bathing costume which mirrored the long, slim, streamlined appearance fashionable for everyday wear. The bulky, tightly-waisted silhouette of the costumes of previous decades disappeared as women adopted a style very similar to the male maillot.

The move towards simplified costumes for women was apparent by 1926 when Laidlaw Leeds, now the Farmers' Trading Company of Auckland, offered a one-piece all-wool suit. It wasn't quite as modern as it sounded — 'one-piece' simply meant it had a skirt attached — but things were definitely loosening up: V necklines were in and sleeves were out, while colour combinations had moved beyond black and navy to include black/cardinal, navy/royal and vieux rose/nil green. Ladies' bathing caps now came in the 'helmet' shape and in 'a good assortment of becoming shades'.

Women's one-piece costumes evolved from those of the late 1920s in which loose-fitting shorts were sewn into the vest-like top, leaving a band around the thigh to give a skirt-like effect. Eventually this band was further reduced in width and then dispensed with altogether. Australian long distance

1920s. If the times didn't yet allow the top half of the costume to be dispensed with, then at least it could be abbreviated as much as scoops and cutouts allowed.

Advertisement from Farmers' Trading Company mail order catalogue for 1925.

swimmer Annette Kellerman was responsible in large part for the adoption of the one-piece suit, wearing a one-piece of her own making — a suit that was not only form-fitting but bared more of the limbs than was the norm — in swimming contests in the years prior to 1910 when the norm was still for multilayered garments. Early one-piece suits derived from her design were known as 'regulation' or 'Annette Kellerman' costumes.

Male bathers in the twenties could choose between two-piece outfits — consisting of trunks worn either under or over a vest — and one-piece, with attached skirt.

By the end of the twenties, women could slip into a striped 'Coney Island' all-wool suit in red, salmon, jade or royal. Brand-new were ladies' porous rubber

A day out at New Brighton, Christchurch, in the 1920s. The increasing popularity of sunbathing would ensure an ongoing demand for more revealing swimsuits.

The first years of the 1910s saw the enveloping dress-style women's costumes being replaced by newer more form-fitting swimsuits — for reasons more obvious to younger women, as this cartoon from an August 1913 issue of *Punch* magazine points out. The older woman, in an old-style costume, comments to the other: 'Really, Gladys, the bathing dresses you girls wear are disgraceful. Look at me; do I show my figure?'

bathing shoes, thoughtfully in shades to tone with the (moulded seamless) caps. Men also had their 'Coney Island' suits, with white tops and black pants,

Or you could choose assorted coloured stripes, and a belt. Belts were 'big' and were to be mainstays of the male outfit for many years. By the early 1930s, the top portion of men's swimsuits was often reduced to thin straps with a bib-like front. Men who were perhaps a little more daring adopted bathing suits which simply consisted of trunks and no vest. Most commonly, these were black with a white webbing belt to hold up the trunks. They could now bare their chests: in 1938 shorts — without vests — were 'right this year'.

The popularity of sunbathing had a major influence on the styling of swimwear in the 1930s. To allow maximum exposure of the body to the sun's rays, swimsuits became more revealing than ever before. Swimsuits such as the 'Roslyn Sunback' were designed with cutout backs and adjustable straps to give the wearer the opportunity 'to make the most of the sun'. The cult of fitness and health in the 1930s further enabled swimsuits to gain cleaner lines, expose more limb and encouraged suits which allowed greater freedom of movement.

The 1930s also saw a new fabric — terry towelling — begin to be used for bathing robes and scarves, and at the same time two local swimsuit brandnames made their mark on the beach: 'Roslyn', whose costumes included the 'semi-sunback', and 'Speedo', whose suits promised 'absolute freedom of movement' in the new fashionable colours of jade, cherry, maroon and orange. Speedo also made swimming suits for men with 'two exclusive, outstanding features': the racer back and half skirt. 'Speedo' togs had been launched in Australia in the mid 1920s as the 'all-Aussie cossie'. Like the first Ford motorcar — available in any colour as long as it was black — the original Speedo cotton-knit swimsuit was available only in navy blue.

Bathing suits were now known as 'swimming suits', and Roslyn marketed them in all-wool elastic knit. They were 'smartly cut, with the new brassiere top' and had 'full sun-back with well-gripping shoulder straps'. Colours included green, scarlet and brick. Elasticised knit fabrics to give a more figure-hugging shape also appeared for the first time.

Beach pyjamas were the fashion in 1934.

'Fun in the sun' swimwear as advertised in the Farmers' Trading Company Catalogue for 1938.

An advertising photograph of the 1940s for Jantzen swimwear. By this time the men's chests were bare, but it would be some years yet before men's, or women's, costumes went below the navel.

Swimsuit evolution: (from left to right) the 'Canadian' suit of the early 1920s; backless costume (1930s); two-piece (1940s); shirred one-piece (1950s); bikini (1960s). The 'Canadian'-style suit was adopted with enthusiasm by women bathers. Its suitability — and potential — were described in an Australian magazine of the time: 'This costume seems specially designed by providence to meet the requirements of feminine bathers,' it said. 'The average girl, when she commences surf-bathing, shrinks from notice, and chooses a costume of amplitude. After a few weeks, she no longer shrinks, but the costume does and gradually assumes proportions at once useful and picturesque.'

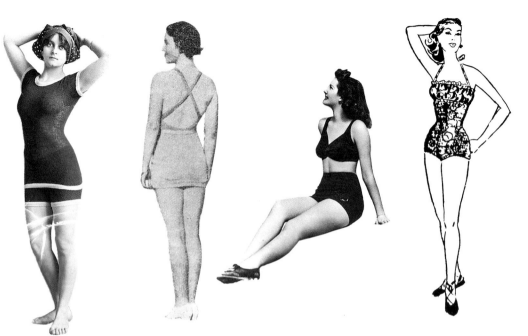

At the end of the thirties, after years of 'Canadian' and 'Coney Island' influence, local manufacturers Roslyn and Canterbury honoured various North Island beaches in their new ranges. Thus 'Miss Milford' featured a shaped bust-line and crossed braid straps, 'Miss Surfdale' was an exotic floral design with two-way straps, 'Miss Manly' featured slimming lines, 'Miss Kawau' a halter neck and flowered patterns, while 'Miss Tauranga' boasted an adjustable brassiere top.

For the next 15 years or so, swimwear designs altered little, but the materials they were made from did, at least in respect of women's swimsuits. While men's togs were still all wool and pepetually soggy women could enjoy printed cottons, chenille and elasticised fabrics.

The fashion for women's swimsuits in the 1950s was to exaggerate the form of the bust which was almost invariably padded or underwired to achieve the fashionable conical or cantilevered look. As well, coincidental with the development of synthetic fibres in this decade, swimwear became more streamlined and close-fitting. New printing techniques meant that patterned fabric came to be more commonly used for swimwear.

The most striking development in women's swimwear in the postwar years was undoubtedly the emergence of the two-piece bathing suit.

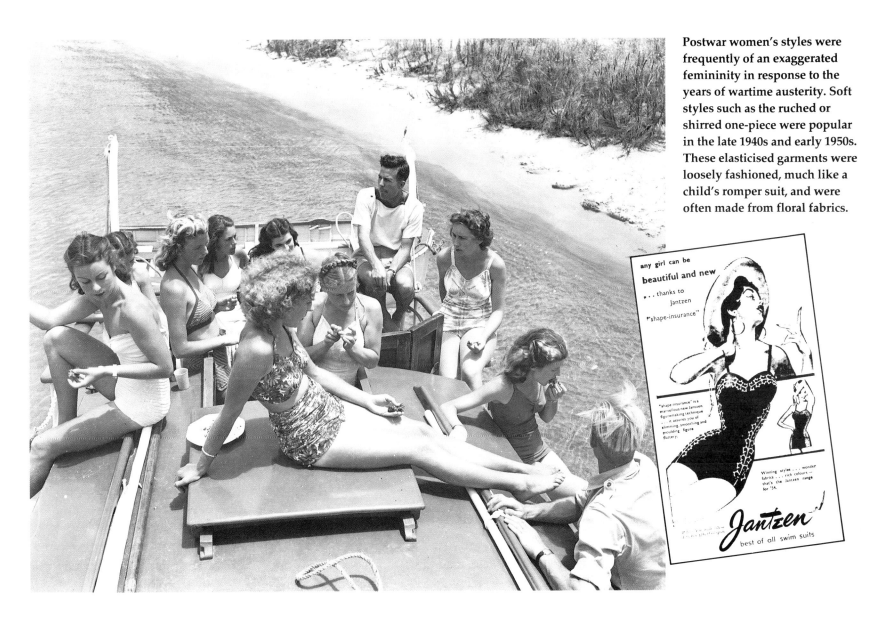

Postwar women's styles were frequently of an exaggerated femininity in response to the years of wartime austerity. Soft styles such as the ruched or shirred one-piece were popular in the late 1940s and early 1950s. These elasticised garments were loosely fashioned, much like a child's romper suit, and were often made from floral fabrics.

The 'two-piece' began to appear on New Zealand beaches in the late 1940s and early 1950s, although it had featured in the fashion press as early as the mid 1930s. The name 'bikini' was coined in 1946, the impact of the swimsuit on the beaches of Europe being likened to that of the nuclear bomb testing then being conducted at Bikini Atoll in the Pacific. (Before the name 'bikini' was confirmed, its designer had first called the new style 'atome'.) The earliest bikini was essentially a swimsuit which left a few inches of bare flesh between the top and bottom. The navel was not exposed until the late 1950s.

The bikini had only modest acceptance on New Zealand beaches through the fifties. Its great popularity had to await the mid sixties when — now considerably briefer, the 'itsy bitsy teeny weeny yellow polka dot bikini' of the song — it was taken up by teenage girls of the baby boom generation, who had both the youthful figure and the attitude to wear it.

The bikini held sway during the 1960s and 1970s, with the one-piece resuming its dominance in the early 1980s. Crochet bikinis were big in the 1970s. Also those with ring fasteners on the tops and sides of the briefs. In New Zealand 'the' place to see the most up-to-date bikini fashions was the Mount, the most popular place for teenagers in the upper half of the North Island.

Men's bathing costumes have been confined over the last 30 years to a choice between brief 'Speedo-type' togs (first introduced in the mid thirties) and boxer or 'baggie' shorts, the latter now pretty much the dominant style for men.

Crochet bikinis were big in the early seventies.

An attraction of the beach is of course the sun. The two don't necessarily go hand in hand, but the country's sunniest spots do tend to be on the coast. Most places in New Zealand average some 2000 hours of sunshine annually, and top of the list are Whakatane, Blenheim, Tauranga, Riwaka (Motueka) and Nelson.

The Victorians weren't known as sunbathers but knew what do if they got too much sun. Early colonists were advised to treat sunstroke by avoiding all intoxicating drinks and dashing cold water over the head and face. A hat was recommended for shade and ventilation, and a further precaution was to carry a cabbage leaf in it!

When sunbathing became the fashion after 1930, the aim was for a deep overall tan and, if you were female, without the ghostly tell-tale images of shoulder and back straps.

The arrival of the summer sun could be a rude shock, resulting in burnt and blistered skin followed by peeling and itching. But with that set-back out of the way — and perhaps relieved by calamine lotion and Q-Tol — the body could now get down to developing a serious tan. Medical science assisted in the search for the fashionable mahogany veneer: 'Coppertone' said it all. Alternatively, many devotees of the sun swore by the traditional coconut oil treatment, its creamy aroma discernible on the sea breeze some considerable distance from where it had been applied.

The effects of excessive exposure to the sun in this country had been observed by at least 1878. In that year an Otago resident travelling in the North Island wrote: 'The vegetation of Tauranga is more tropical than that of Otago. Bamboos grow with luxuriance. The people, however, are sunburnt and prematurely dried up. Yet they are in raptures with the climate, and pitied us south-landers.'

Charles Brasch recalls his youthful appetite for a tan: 'We prized our freedom most, perhaps, because it gave us time to sit in the sun. We were sun worshippers. The Oamaru air is clear, but winters there are sharp and cold easterlies spoil many a fine day; the sun was never too much with us. We loved baring our bodies to it and to each other; we admired sun-burnt bodies and despised white ones and spent long hours carefully darkening our skins with the aid of creams and lotions. . . . We did not wear clothes to hide our bodies; and naked, we were fully clothed in nakedness, which was perfectly natural to us.'

Boys' SUN HELMETS 1/6 EACH

F1398—Made in four shades: Khaki Grey, and Navy. Necessary for summer Exactly as illustrated. Sizes, 6¼ to 7. Price, 1/6 each.

STRAWS

No. F1404— BOYS' VENTILATED STRAW HATS.—Sizes, 6¼ to 6⅞. Price, 1/- each.

The Sunlight League's poster of the 1930s set down some simple rules to follow if sunbathers were to enjoy the benefits of the 'sunbath'.

Oriental Bay, Wellington, and not a tube of sunblock to be seen. (1951)

In 1940 a beauty columnist wrote that 'Nothing is quite so young looking as a good tan'. The 1940 advice was to use the sun intelligently, and begin the process gently. The sun was regarded as some sort of cosmic cure-all: 'Impregnate your system with the sun-vitamin, and not only will you insure it against common colds, but you will have a substitute for the vitamins found in dairy and other fats'.

During war-time restrictions the sun was a handy ally in the battle for health. For those who overdid the cure, relief was provided by witch-hazel, cotton or linen pads soaked in buttermilk, or even baking powder piled on the badly burned parts.

Sunlight *is*, of course, a vital ingredient in good health, helping in the formation of vitamin D, necessary for healthy teeth and bones. Fresh air and sunshine were enthusiastically endorsed by the Plunket Society for New Zealand's expectant mothers and their unborn babies. When baby came along there were 12 essentials for successful 'modern mothercraft', and fresh air and sunshine were top of the list. The recommended sunbathing procedure was to choose a sheltered spot, preferably before 10 am or after 3 pm in the summer. Baby was to be exposed progressively to achieve an even tan, and with a sturdy hat to protect the eyes and back of the neck.

Plunket advised mothers that children who spent too much time indoors had a 'washed-out' appearance, lacking the 'vim and vigour of outdoor boys and girls'. Systematic sunbathing was an essential feature of a child's daily programme during summer. But more than that, Plunket recommended that the sun should be taken at the beach: 'Whenever possible children should be taken for excursions to the beach in the summer.'

When, in the late 1980s, New Zealand learned its protective ozone layer had diminished, the days of carefree tanning were over. Now, the fear of melanoma stalks the beaches. In the early 1970s radio stations had provided a roll-over service for evenly tanned listeners, but in the '90s the advice is to get out of the sun altogether.

Children of the twenties wore covering swimsuits in the interests of modesty, but today — along with a sunhat and sunblock — it's a matter of health. Too much sun can kill.

Children from Otaki Health Camp enjoy a dip in the sea, 1945. Sea, sun and fresh air—cornerstones of the Health Camp ethos—were all to be enjoyed at the beach.

The circle has come full turn, so that the wide-brimmed hats, limb-covering summer clothing and parasols of the turn of the century are to be seen once more on our beaches, and so-called 'burn times' are well-heeded. These are simplified calculations that err on the side of caution in trying to create awareness among all of the population, not just beachgoers, of the dangers presented by being out in the noonday sun. With the thinning of the earth's protective ozone layer, prolonged exposure to the heat of the summer sun is positively dangerous. Burn times result from combining data on expected ozone levels with weather forecasts to provide maximum exposure times, these times based on the sun's effect on a completely untanned Caucasian. So that a burn time of 20 minutes means that such a sample skin will show noticeable reddening after 20 minutes under a noonday sun.

While it is true that a tan provides protection against sun damage, it is again a matter of those who tan most easily obtaining the greatest protection. While sunscreen lotions will enable one to extend the time in the sun, it is more sensible to limit the amount of time your skin is exposed. But it can be hard to break old habits, when for three generations or more 'summer' and 'beach' have been synonymous with 'tan'. Indeed the allure of the golden tan is so ingrained that it will take perhaps a further generation for habits to change, although on today's beaches the evidence, in terms of the greater number of hats being worn and the use of sunblocks, particularly in the case of children, indicates that the message is getting through. And, in fact, it is with children that the issue is most critical, research showing that the greatest damage by the sun to the skin takes place in the first ten years of one's life.

Beauty contests, in which 'beauty and the beach' came together, began in the 1930s and enjoyed their heyday in the 1950s and 1960s. Held at numerous beach resorts throughout the country during the Christmas-New Year holiday period, these contests are run by local boroughs or community groups, often in association with local businesses, at halls or open-air venues such as soundshells. They are contests that have managed over the years to maintain an inoffensive wholesomeness, a quality demonstrated by the time it took for the bikini to become acceptable swimwear for a contest winner. A 1967 *Weekly News* article on beauty contests revealed what judges were looking for: 'On the subject of why brunettes should do well, one girl volunteered the thought that "perhaps the judges feel rather doubtful about blondes today because their apparently genuine hair-colour can so easily come out of a bottle."

'Judges do not seem to be specifically asked to weigh in on the side of the natural, rather than the artificially assisted beauty, but in New Zealand they strongly incline to do so anyway. False eyelashes and heavy eye make-up meet generally with a cool reception, teeth are carefully observed, and questions are often asked as to whether or not a girl does her hair herself or is mainly dependent upon the hairdresser.

'Again, although there is rarely any ruling about the wearing of bikinis, which are accepted beach wear after all, judges here seem to be "agin" them and the girl who wears one in a bathing beauty contest appears to put herself at a distinct disadvantage.'

The first outdoor contest was held at Mount Maunganui in 1946. Also famous for its outdoor venue is Caroline Bay.

Contestants in the 1956 Miss Caroline Bay bathing beauty contest.

B *the*  SEASIDE

Beside the Seaside

BY THE END OF THE 1920s the beach was firmly established as the favourite recreational destination for New Zealanders. And two weeks on the sand over summer was the preferred end-of-year annual holiday. The following three decades was to see that reputation consolidated and the flowering of a widely shared beach culture. Beachgoing had become an integral part of national life.

'Caroline Bay! What memories surge up in the minds of those whose privilege it has been to visit this popular holiday resort.' (From an enthusiastic visitors' guide to Timaru, published by the Caroline Bay Association, 1929.)

One of the joys of the beach is the chance to enjoy the benefits of nature. In most cases the beachgoer has the persistent forces of wind and water to thank for the varied nature of the coastline. But there is one New Zealand beach for which nature cannot take full credit. At Timaru, it was human intervention which eventually resulted in the formation of Caroline Bay and, at various times, its self-styled claims to the titles 'Riviera of New Zealand' and 'Venice of the South'.

Thanks to the Bay, Timaru could also call itself 'the most attractive of the sea-board towns of New Zealand'. This was a far cry from 1830 when the area was a whaling station, supplied by a ship named *Caroline*.

Timaru began life as an isolated village scattered along a boisterous coast. It was difficult—and dangerous—to approach from the sea, and the site of many wrecks. Things improved with the start of harbour construction in 1870, and seven years later work began on a breakwater. A dramatic by-product of this was reclamation caused by the build-up of shingle deposits to the south of the breakwater, this new land later becoming the railway yards. But the coastal current also deposited smaller particles to the north, and eventually the sandy sweep of Caroline Bay was formed, the efforts of humans capitalised on by the mechanics of the sea, with swimmers and holiday-

'Silvery sanded' Caroline Bay: this photograph is from the 1920s when Japanese-style parasols, of oiled paper or cotton, were in fashion.

makers the beneficiaries ever since.

The potential of the beach was recognised by a Bay improvement scheme as early as 1897. On the then statutory half-holiday in each week, volunteer 'working bees' attacked the cliffs to convert them into lawn and garden. The effort snowballed, and the need for further improvements brought about the formation of the Caroline Bay Association. Tentative Christmas Carnivals were held as fund-raisers, and their grow-

Beside the sea at St Clair Beach, Dunedin. Its saltwater swimming pool (pictured here at the far end of the beach) was opened in 1883 — one of many built throughout the country at this period to meet the demand created by the interest in leisure-time sporting pursuits.

ing success and additional improvements soon resulted in Timaru's — and one of the country's — 'chief pleasure grounds'.

Certainly, the Caroline Bay Association was never short of praise for its growing asset — 'a vast stretch of sand, shelving gently to form a resting place for the waters of the Pacific'. Here, in 1929, 'youths and maidens [enjoyed] life to the full in the luke warm surf or basking in the sunshine'. But there was more to it than just lying around on the beach: 'For those who are run down in health and who have been ordered a complete rest, no finer haven could be provided than Caroline Bay bathed in sunshine.' It was promoted as a year-round attraction: 'Open ... to the cool breezes in the summer' and 'snugly sheltered from the cold southerly blast in the winter'.

But the main attraction was clearly the quality of the bathing: 'Nowhere in this country can this half-mile stretch of firm, clear sand, which shelves smoothly and gradually, be equalled.' Here the waters could be as placid as a lake, and at other times the swell was 'just sufficient to lift the bather joyously on to the crest of the wave with a new sense of elation'. And for those whose health did not 'permit of a glad romp with the sea', the ever enterprising Bay Association provided hot sea-water baths nearby.

'Silvery sanded' Caroline Bay had it all. To encourage beachgoers to take the train there in the 1930s, New Zealand Railways advertised the place as 'peerless'. And for good reason — not only could Caroline Bay claim to be one of the most popular, safe and attractive beaches in the land, but it provided a staggering range of amenities. By the mid sixties it was probably New Zealand's best equipped piece of coastal development, covering more than fifty acres (22 hectares). Over the years it included lawns, gardens and shrubberies, playing fields, tennis and basketball courts, tennis pavilion with grandstand roof, band rotunda, paddling pools, picnic areas (with gas rings), Sound

Shell, hall, a stadium seating 5000, tea rooms, aviary, roller skating rink, pony rides, bathing sheds and diving raft. And if that wasn't enough, every Christmas beachgoers could enjoy a 'complete carnival programme.'

Over the Christmas period, daily concert party performances took place in the Sound Shell and dances were held every night (except Sundays) in the hall. For the energetic holidaymaker there were races, for the creative there were sand-modelling contests (entry forms published in the *Weekly News*), and for animal lovers, pet parades. The latter were open to all-comers except dogs, canines being excluded from the Bay on account of city by-laws. For families there were Mother-and-Son as well as Mother-and-Daughter contests. In both cases Mum was required to appear in a 'sunsuit' (as opposed to a swimming costume), as was daughter (to be aged between 3 and 6 years), while son was to wear bathing shorts. The very young were eligible for the Tiny Tots parades.

For the beauty-conscious there was a whole range of competitions. Single or married aspirants aged over 14 had the chance to be Queen of the Carnival and take home £75. Hopefuls had to come prepared, to appear successively in street wear ('frock — no hats'), sunsuits (shorts and tops), casual wear, the inevitable bathing costume and, finally, evening wear.

Future beauty queens may well have gained valuable experience by entering the Princess of the Sands contest. For this, entrants had to be between 9 and 13 years old, and the winner collected £10 as well as the considerable honour of being attendant to the Queen of the Carnival. But the glamour event of the whole holiday period was undoubtedly the Miss Caroline Bay Bathing Beauty Contest. This was open to single women over the age of 16, and they appeared in bathing costume, with footwear optional. While first prize of £40 was considerably less than that awarded

New Brighton Pier, Christchurch. The pier — 210 metres long — was built in 1896 in the hope that this beach suburb might become a resort like its English namesake.

Happy days at Waipu Cove

Holidaymakers, with young people in the majority, found a pleasant spot for the festive season at Waipu Cove, Northland. The ocean beach was well patronised and beauty contests attracted many entrants.

The finalists in the beauty contest. From left are Miss Jocelyn Taine (Miss Waipu Cove, 1955), Miss Joan Barnett (second) and Miss Maureen Gould (third)

Competitors in the junior beauty contest

The beauty contest was a highlight of the Christmas holiday at Waipu Cove as well.

to the Carnival Queen, the Bathing Beauty did get free air tickets to the national 'Miss New Zealand Resorts' contest. In 1966 this was held at the Mount, and it offered another £100 for the winner.

Holiday fun at Caroline Bay traditionally began on Boxing Day and no doubt a highlight of the season was the midnight bonfire on New Year's Eve. Then, after a Saturday night dance from 8 pm to midnight a couple of weeks later, it was all over for another year.

Apart from surfing, whose hardy followers seem to carry on regardless of the weather, recreation at the beach is usually associated with sunshine. The parts of New Zealand most favoured by the sun — those receiving over 2350 hours annually — are near Blenheim, the Tasman Bay area from Nelson to Riwaka, and the Bay of Plenty near Whakatane. Not far behind, at over 2000 hours per year, are Central Otago and coastal parts of Gisborne and Hawke's Bay. Therefore, that bit of New Zealand which seems to possess the best combination of sun and sea is the northern tip of the South Island. For good reason, then, this has been termed the 'Sunshine Coast'. It even possesses a Golden Bay, although this name does not refer to sunshine, or the tobacco grown in the area, but to the valuable mineral once discovered there. And it is Nelson in particular which can lay the earliest claim to a hot sun, even if recent statistics don't entirely support it.

In 1842 Edward Gibbon Wakefield observed New Zealand Company immigrants coming ashore at Nelson and noted: 'The sun was hotter than I have ever felt before'. Nearly a century later—in the 1930s—the Nelson Provincial Progress League claimed the city's average sunshine record of 2545 hours per annum was higher than that of any other town in New Zealand—or 'Great Britain or sunny Italy' for that matter—and beat Sydney, Melbourne and Adelaide to boot. To provide international resort comparison, Bournemouth and Torquay were quoted as only being able to muster 1796 and 1759 hours respectively.

Curiously, neighbouring Blenheim was accredited with only 2171 hours, suggesting some considerable changes on the meteorological front since, as the national record for annual sunshine hours is now firmly held by Blenheim — with an all-time high of 2686 hours in 1972. It can also claim the country's three sunniest-ever months: January 1957, December 1974

A big blow at Tahunanui beach, Nelson. 'Surfing' then described body-surfing and the use of shortish boards to 'shoot the breakers'. Surfing as we know it today, using long boards, began to be seen around the 1930s.

and November 1968, in that order.

In spite of any statistics to the contrary, Nelson has long enjoyed the prefix of 'Sunny' and status as capital of the 'Sunshine Coast'. Its chief asset in this respect is Tahunanui — known locally simply as Tahuna — a residential suburb and seaside resort close to the city centre. Nelson's most popular beach, it is also considered one of the finest in the country, combining gently sloping sands with unusually large tides and safe swimming. Shallow water here ensures no wild surf or undertow, and the tides captured within Tasman Bay are gently warmed by the sun.

Tahunanui translates as 'many sandbanks' and lies on the southeast shore of Tasman Bay. On the opposite side of this indentation is another beach resort, Kaiteriteri. Here, 1950s tourist publicity claimed, 'golden sands' was no fanciful misnomer, and this beach was for those seeking 'sun, sea and serenity'. It also offers surfers a beach break, best at high tide with a northwest swell.

Elsewhere on Tasman Bay are the beaches of Rabbit Island (accessible by road bridge), Ruby Bay (good for surfing), Kina (offering sheltered swimming and water-skiing), Motueka, Sandy Bay and Marahau. Surfing in the area also includes a good right reef break at the Cut, at Nelson Harbour, although a lengthy paddle is required to catch it.

Westwards from Nelson is Golden Bay itself, protected from the north by the 24-kilometre long Farewell Spit, on the southern shore of which is Pohara, described thus in 1937: 'It is almost impossible to exaggerate the beauty of this spot. A lovely curve of golden sands, from which rise bush-clad hills'. Further to the north, Pakawau and Puponga provide swimming and boating facilities, and there are also recognised beaches at Totaranui, Tata, Ligar Bay, Partons Rock and Collingwood.

In the Marlborough Sounds with its hundreds of kilometres of indented coastline, fiords and beaches, is some of the country's most spectacular scenery. Some parts are accessible only by boat.

'Having a ripping time at Wellington'– a postcard from around 1910. Cheap picture postcards first appeared in the 1890s. The well known risqué cards of the British seaside never really had a New Zealand equivalent.

Evans Bay, Wellington, 1930s. Men's and women's costumes are still woollen, but now briefer and, in the case of women's suits, backless.

Cape Foulwind, Buller, 1910s: excursionists on the beach for a day out. By the turn of the century the beach had established itself as a popular holiday destination — the merge of sea and sand an irresistible attraction.

Such secluded beaches are a far cry from New Zealand's usual coastal playgrounds. The holiday resorts of The Portage and Kenepuru offer numerous holiday spots and camping sites. Pelorus Sound caters for boating, fishing, picnicking and swimming, Queen Charlotte Sound similarly.

For surfing, however, one needs to go to Cloudy Bay on the Pacific coast, where sandy beaches also enable good surfcasting and hand-line fishing. Further south is Mangamaunu, a wild open beach that attracts surfers to its consistently good right pointbreak. Marfell Beach offers fishing, camping and safe swimming. This coast is well endowed with beaches, although they can be hazardous. But then you can always stay clear of the water altogether and instead try a bonfire of driftwood, complete with barbecued local crayfish. Finally, for our purposes, is Kaikoura, whose very name (translated as 'meal of crayfish') reflects the richness of the seacoast. The beginnings of European settlement here were due to the whaling industry, and it is the observation of whales and other marine mammals that have recently given this community a new lease of life.

A caravan party at Goose Bay, Kaikoura, 1947: as close to heaven as one might get.

Various holiday spots in New Zealand may squabble over which is sunniest, but there is no doubt about the area that sees the sun first each day. Weather permitting, this honour goes to Hikurangi, a 1754-metre peak in the Raukumara Range overlooking the East Cape of the North Island, and handy to a large number of beaches.

A journey around East Cape might appropriately commence in the Bay of Plenty, taking in the sandy sweep from the Mount through to Opotiki. The latter is noted for safe sandy beaches suitable for swimming and surf-casting, and nearby are those of Waiotahi and Hukuwai.

The main road eastwards winds around some spectacular cliff-top views of the coast and provides many opportunities for campers. The main settlement in this district is Te Kaha, famous for its fishing, a resource apparent to European whalers as early as the 1830s. Around the Cape, beaches and camping spots come thick and fast. This was the region, according to enthusiastic tourist literature in the 1960s, that 'New Zealanders themselves flock to in summer; their caravans and tents dot the little bays, their boats explore the richest of sea-fishing waters, and their families enjoy the freedom of long summer days by pohutukawa-fringed beaches'.

Alternatively, another writer claimed these beaches presented 'a bewildering variety of quaint coves, sheltered bays and brief, snowy beaches which almost

demand that you camp on them'. It was imaginative to compare the glistening sands of these shores with their geographical opposite — snow!

As for pohutukawas, the oldest and largest specimen of this tree is to be found at Te Araroa, near Hicks Bay. Known as Te Waha-o-Rerekohu, this monster was well underway when Captain Cook visited the East Cape in 1769. Nowadays it boasts some 22 separate branches and a canopy extending almost 40 metres.

Napier, 1908: swimming attire may have become less formal but you still dressed up to go to the beach. But then adults at least were 'dressed up' most of the time. (Among the bowler hats can be seen a couple of straw boaters, a new fashion at this time.)

Near the top of the Cape is Waihau Bay, whose broad shingly beach extends northeastwards to Cape Runaway, and is excellent for camping and sea fishing. The road along this route offers travellers, again according to a 1960s writer, 'an overwhelming magnificence of coastal scenery unsurpassed anywhere'. Camping sites are also to be found on nearby Whangaparaoa Bay, but consent is necessary from local land owners.

From this point State Highway 35 turns inland and avoids the coast. Apart from Hicks Bay and Te Araroa, the Pacific is not encountered again until Tokomaru Bay, on the East Coast proper. The bay is rich in Maori history, its name honouring one of the ancestral canoes. Much later, Captain James Cook and his botanists from the *Endeavour* came ashore here to collect specimens. Nowadays the principal business — apart from swimming and fishing — is sheep-farming, a derelict freezing works being stark evidence of a changed economy.

From Tokomaru Bay the main road south goes inland, emerging from the hilly country at Tolaga Bay. Here, at Cooks Cove, the famous mariner called in for water and other supplies, including some vital 'greens'.

The East Coast's best — or, at least, most populous — beaches are found at Gisborne, some 56 kilometres southwest of Tolaga Bay. The coastline here boasts some of the finest surf in the country, and this feature wasn't lost on Captain Cook either. Journals of the intrepid explorer contain numerous references to heavy surf preventing landings on shore. Two centuries later, this area is also noted for its colonies of holiday houses, with the added bonus of crimson clouds of flowering pohutukawa during the Christmas period.

The East Coast road meets the Pacific again at the popular summer camping spot of Pouawa. But diversions off state highway 35 also give access to Waihau Bay and Whangara, both worthy beaches. Closer to Gisborne are Tatapouri (famous for its crayfishing)

Ngamotu Beach was among the 'glorious beaches' promoted to visitors to New Plymouth. (1910)

'Under the pohutukawa', whose flowers herald the New Zealand Christmas.

and the beach-cottage settlement of Makorori. Southwest of here is Wainui Beach, whose name translates appropriately as 'big waters'. From the sandhills overlooking this long curving beach swimmers and surfers can contemplate thunderous breakers crashing in on the white sands.

Captain Cook may have been a great navigator, but he made a big mistake when naming the bay south of Gisborne. His disastrous encounter there with the local Maori population understandably inspired 'Poverty Bay', but it is a definite misnomer if beaches are taken into account. One writer in the 1930s suggested 'Bountiful Bay' as an alternative, no doubt in deference to Waikanae and Midway. Both beaches boast motor camps with cabins, camp sites and caravan parks, while Waikanae offers not only surfing and golden sands but the chance to rent a cell for the night — the Churchill Park Motor Camp being on the site of the old Gisborne jail. Gisborne has been described as being 'reminiscent of Caroline Bay at Timaru', perhaps on account of its sheltering harbour mole. The same writer was also pleased to report that — in 1936 anyway — Gisborne beaches were free of one of his tribal enemies as a sunbather — the sandfly.

'Summer' means 'holiday', and for most New Zealanders a summer holiday at the beach. By the 1910s the country's coastal towns and cities found themselves with a real asset, and weren't backward in promoting their charms to the rest of the country.

Between the western Bay of Plenty and the Hauraki Gulf lies the rugged peninsula of Coromandel. In terms of beaches, this spit of land can be seen as a sort of microcosm of New Zealand. On its western side, protected by the Firth of Thames, are sheltered beaches ideal for children and yachts, while across the ranges to the east is the blue Pacific playground of more adventurous swimmers, surfers, deepsea fishermen and surfcasters.

Coromandel is increasingly the retreat of Aucklanders in search of a holiday- or weekend-home. It simply requires a lefthand turn at the bottom of the Bombay Hills and a quick drive over the Hauraki Plains, although travel on the peninsula itself is a little more demanding; its rugged vertebra is negotiated by four main roads linking its opposite coasts. It might seem more like an island than a peninsula, and a circumnavigation of its numerous beaches would appropriately begin at Waihi.

This district owes its beginnings to gold — in the early 1900s the Martha Mine was the eleventh richest in the world — but now it has other attractions. Waihi Beach, originally intended as a retirement home for miners, is a combined residential and resort area some 8 kilometres from Waihi township. Its 10 kilometres of Pacific beach frontage provide for baches, swimming, surfing, and fishing.

On the Pacific coast, Coromandel really begins at

Donkey rides, Waihi Beach, 1948.

Whangamata, its name meaning 'obsidian harbour', a reference to the prized black volcanic rock obsidian washed ashore here from Mayor Island and utilised by the Maori for tool-making.

Whangamata was once something of a quiet retreat, but — like Waihi — now undergoes a major summer transformation. It is geographically favoured by a choice of beaches — on a river estuary or the ocean. The latter provides three recognised surfing spots, at the Estuary, Beach and Bar. And north and south of Whangamata — from Opoutere to Whiritoa — are beaches noted for their varied opportunities, from surfcasting to swimming, floundering and shellfishing, or just picnicking under the shade of pohutukawas.

Time was when Whangamata was the traditional holiday spot for prosperous dairy farmers from the Hauraki Plains. But in recent years even they may not have been able to keep pace with the type of holiday homes springing up on the western side of the peninsula. In particular there is Pauanui, a town whose permanent population is in the hundreds but rockets into five figures during the summer. The name of this rapidly growing seaside settlement means many or large (nui) shellfish (paua), but the area is more obviously characterised by its numerous (and large) holiday homes. Few of these would qualify as 'baches' in the traditional sense of the word, with Pauanui's amenities — which include an airfield and golf links — putting the town into the 'resort' category.

Long before Pauanui was discovered, neighbouring Tairua was a favourite for surfers because of its beach break. Directly across the harbour from Pauanui — but a 29 kilometre trip by road — Tairua's highlights include the climb to the top of Paku, the twin-peaked knoll on Tokoroa Point overlooking the entrance to Tairua Harbour. From the top one has the spectacular sight of the inlet, its waters changing in colour with varying depth and materials.

Sandhill campers at Hahei beach, Coromandel Peninsula, 1961.

At Hotwater Beach, 50 kilometres north of Whangamata, hot water seeps through the volcanic sand, enabling beachgoers to scoop out their own spa pools. This attraction is only possible between low and mid tides, and temperature increases with the depth of the diggings. Bathers are directed across the Tauwaiwe Stream to dig 'between the cliff and the sea-girt rock'. Surely there can be few beaches anywhere in the world offering a swim in the surf followed by a gentle sulphurous steam bath in a sandy foxhole.

A little north of Hotwater Beach is Hahei, a beach tinted pink with crushed shells. This seaside locality is popular with skindivers, and also offers the spectacular sight of blow-holes and the sea-carved Cathedral Cove. And around the corner towards Whitianga is another locality with scope for boating, swimming and fishing and memories of a famous visitor here on 5 November 1769 — Cooks Beach.

Whitianga itself looks out over what has been described as an 'emerald estuary'. Mercury Bay can boast a 'golden coronet' of no less than 40 kilometres of beaches. Adjacent to Whitianga is Buffalo Beach, named after Her Majesty's ship that fell foul to an easterly gale here in 1840. Nowadays this stretch of sand is used for swimming, water skiing and surfing, as is nearby Wharekaho Bay (or Simpsons Beach). The latter is also well-known to surfcasters and shell collectors alike and possesses a clump of ancient and huge pohutukawa trees. Other beaches in the vicinity of Mercury Bay include Rings, Matarangi and Brophys and the more curiously named Front and Lonely.

With the arrival of Europeans in Coromandel, kauri forests were stripped and hillsides scarred by gold-seekers. Along with the new settlers, introduced plants and animals took hold. But just north of Whitianga is a remnant of New Zealand before this impact. The sandy stretches of Otama Beach are considered the best remaining pristine dunes in the country. Thanks only to their comparative isolation, the original native plant cover of these dunes is largely intact, making it a significant area for ecological research. By 1993 the Department of Conservation and the local District Council had acquired most of the 16 hectares of dunes as a protected reserve.

Useful beaches and bays are also to be found on

> **HOLIDAY ACCOMMODATION**
> BACHES, seaside, furn., fishing, swimming. Vacancies available. Ph. Ak. 24-126. or write Mannion and Morris, Coromandel. k
> BEAUTIFULLY situated modern fully furn. s.c. hol flats open fire comfort; children welcome Deepacre, Takapuna. Ph. 78-502. k
> HOLIDAY or honeymoon, popular and economical in a modern caravan hired from 69 Marlow Rd. Christchurch. E.3. k
> MT Maunganui. Longwood cabins Enjoy winter vac. in N.Z.'s mildest climate comf. accom., reduced winter rent, reductions for pensioners K. Dyer. Box 25. Ph 347. k
> ROTORUA. Haupapa St. The Lynwood Guest House, friendly and home atmosphere, offering all the essential amenities. Comfort. home cooking, own mineral bath. Central. Dinner, bed, breakfast. 21/-. Resident proprietors, Major and Mrs C. F. A. Wagstaff. Ph. Rotorua. 954. k
> TAKAPUNA Beach. S.C. flats, every conv., includ. frig. and radio. Specially built for the discriminating holidaymaker. Marvellous outlook Send for illustrated brochure. Takapuna Tourist Court. Box 16 Takapuna Ph 79-240. jg

Under canvas along Front Beach in Whitianga in 1913. The high tide is quite literally at the doorstep.

Mount Maunganui, 'before'.

the northern extremity and west coast of the Coromandel. Tapu, at the western foot of the main range, offers good sea-fishing and camping, while Coromandel township itself is noted for its boating and fishing. Otherwise, camping, boating, fishing and swimming are possible at Waikawau and Fletchers and Kennedys Bay — the latter notable for its crayfishing — and Colville and Port Charles. One enthusiast wrote of the Coromandel's 'glorious beaches divided into separate coves by orange, yellow and flame coloured bluffs, fantastically sculptured into craggy profiles and tasselled with scarlet pohutukawas generously throwing their shade onto the sand below'. The backdrop to this 'golden lining of the Pacific beaches' being, of course, the sea, 'flowing like an endless aquamarine carpet to the far horizon'. Little wonder that by the early 1970s the Coromandel was being promoted as a 'pocket wonderland' and was fast becoming the playground of Auckland and the Waikato.

In November 1769 Captain James Cook's investigation of New Zealand took him around the East Cape and into a large crescent-shaped bay. Finding it well-endowed with provisions, and blessed with an agreeable climate and an hospitable Maori population, he named it the Bay of Plenty — in sharp contrast to his earlier experience at Poverty Bay. At the western end of the bay with the bounteous name is its main centre of Tauranga, and 20 kilometres distant is its major holiday resort, generally known as 'the Mount'.

Tauranga sits on a peninsula between two estuaries — the Waikareao and the Waimapu. It has a natural affinity with the sea and a long history as a holiday spot. While the whole Bay of Plenty has no shortage of sunshine, it was Tauranga that once adopted the slogan 'where the sunshine spends the winter'. And it was Viscount Bledisloe, Governor-General of New Zealand from 1930-35, who described the place as the 'Riviera of the South'.

At the time Tauranga was described as a town divided between 'holidaymakers, retired colonels and dairy farmers'. In summer the former somewhat upset the balance, and certain permanent residents may not have been sad at the end of the season to observe the departure of 'the unrestful tide of young women in slacks and young men in shorts and sandshoes'.

Across the harbour from Tauranga is Mount Maunganui, and one of the country's finest ocean beaches. On the eastern side of the peninsula — which ends in the 232-metre volcanic cone of Mt Maunganui itself — is a beach famous for its surf, while the western side provides a sheltered beach for boats.

Sandcastle competition, Mount Maunganui beach, January 1949. Christmas-New Year 'carnivals' at many of the country's beach resorts continue to have holiday programmes which include similar entertainments — fun runs, community barbecues, discos and competitions.

By the 1930s the Mount had a sizeable reputation for 'surf-bathing'. It was then already a fashionable destination, as writer Robin Hyde (Iris Wilkinson) described in an article in a 1936 issue of the *New Zealand Railways Magazine*:

'Enter a melon party. When I said I didn't know what this meant, everyone looked blanker than ever, which was in itself no mean achievement. The apparent course of Nature is that you wear a bathing suit (a backless one preferred), or at most, shorts, and the new sort of shirt with the zip fastener, and then proceed to get through any amount of pink-fleshed crisp melon.

'You're expected to be able to absorb vast quantities before complaining of that full feeling. Everybody was doing it. They seem to find it aided both conversation and their sun tan, about which last they were a little anxious. This, of course, was at the Mount — I will, though it is against the unwritten local law, give that sugarloaf its full name and address it as Mount Maunganui.

'Sun-tanning was the thing that you simply couldn't hang back from doing; some boated, some swam, some disported themselves in the loveliest cream surf, which appeared in large fat billows and dashed prancing and snorting up the beach. Seagulls, dogs and an occasional infant — not very many, the Mount isn't what I'd call a family-gathering resort — chorussed deep-throated approval. But even those of us who didn't intend to get a little toe wet, submitted ourselves to the enthusiastic embraces of the gorgeous Tauranga sunshine, which is definitely A grade. I saw a well-known professor, who had gone a pale honey-brown practically all over. He was a strange sight, pleasing, although bald.'

Another visitor to the Mount in the late 1930s described the local landmark as a 'frowning bastion', its blue silhouette occurring in all Tauranga landscapes. Appropriately, from a distance it was likened to 'a sand castle turned out carelessly from a child's tin bucket'. At the base of the Mount were sand dunes, pine trees and sea grass, and a random scattering of holiday homes. Their green, red and orange roofs and shutters reputedly gave the place a picturesque and somewhat foreign appearance, as Viscount Bledisloe himself had observed. At the south-eastern foot of the Mount was Pilot Bay, home to a fleet of pleasure craft. In summer all this was supplemented by a colony of mushroom-like tents.

The beach itself was the scene of swimmers in exotic bathing costumes dragging 'gaily painted surfboards', ice cream stalls, reluctant donkeys giving rides to children, and sunbathers burned either as 'dark as Indians' or as 'red as lobsters'. There was definitely a touch of class on this beach: 'languorous ladies' in beach pyjamas sat round under sun umbrellas, and tea-baskets provided welcome refreshment.

While Tauranga's Riviera-like summer charm was appreciated by hordes of beachgoers in the 1930s, even the winter there was not to be overlooked. The ice cream sellers may have shut up shop, the donkeys

---

VISITORS TO WAIHI

SUCCESSFUL HOLIDAY SEASON

There was a large crowd in Waihi on Christmas Eve, and more money was spent than for several years. The number of people at Waihi Beach broke all records. All accommodation houses and cottages were taxed to capacity by 1800 people, while a further 700 were accommodated in tents on the camping area. There were also numerous daily visitors.

A sea of cars, caravans and canvas at the Mount, 1962. The beach culture in full flower.

been left to regain their strength on the slopes of the Mount and easterlies raged across the harbour, sending spray across the waterfront to lash the shops and throw seaweed up on the now deserted beach, but it could still be described as 'sun-drenched'.

By the early 1970s the annual invasion of the Mount — by New Zealanders from all parts of the country — had built to a gloriously hectic army that began its major assault on Boxing Day. According to one on-the-spot description the sight was one of: 'family groups towing caravans, hikers with a tent in their pack, bronzed launch owners with a boat full of big-game gear, teenagers with surf boards strapped to their hot rods'. Over the next four weeks the Mount's then permanent population of 9000 would quadruple, with the overflow drawn to 'the most famous mile of

New Zealand coastline', that sweep of beach running from Mt Maunganui to Moruriki Island — packing out motor camps and motels from Waihi to Opotiki. These were 'sun and outdoor fun worshippers' attracted to the playgrounds of the 'Tourist Diamond of the Pacific'. No doubt many booked into the Papamoa Holiday Camp, about 12 kilometres southeast of the Mount. This then offered tent sites and cabins, including a modern camp kitchen equipped with electric hotplates and Zip tea-maker, not to mention a clean ablutions block, camp store and public 'phone. In addition, there were 65 power points available for caravanners.

North of Tauranga is the seaside resort of Waihi Beach, and eastwards the Bay of Plenty provides an almost continuous sweep of beaches. In particular there is Ohope, Whakatane's resort suburb, which commands some 15 kilometres of sandy shoreline. The western end of the beach is recognised by surfriders for its left point break which holds up to 6-metre high waves. An additional attraction of this area at Christmas-time is the blossoming pohutukawa trees.

Among New Zealand's many beaches is one that may well be the world's longest. But, ironically, it is not nearly as long as it thinks it is. On the west coast of the most northerly and narrowest portion of the North Island — the Aupouri Peninsula — extending from Ahipara at its southern end to Scott Point in the north, is the extensive sandy stretch of Ninety Mile Beach. The origin of the name is something of a mystery, perhaps the result of a miscalculation or simple exaggeration, for in fact the beach is no more than 64 miles (103 kilometres) at its longest.

The original Maori name for this sweep of sand was Te Oneroa a Tohe — 'the long beach of Tohe', in honour of a famous chief. Tohe was the ancestor of the Aupouri tribe which still owns much of the land in the area, and was regarded as the first person to have travelled the beach. The area is rich in Maori lore, for it was northwards up this coast that ancient spirits of the dead paddled their way to Cape Reinga, literally the 'place of leaping', before descending to the underworld. The beach has also been the scene of much bloodshed between northern Aupouri tribes and their constant enemies, the Rarawa of Ahipara in the south, the last battle being fought about 1840.

Abel Tasman passed this way in 1643, and in 1769 the beach's sand dunes inspired James Cook to label it a desert coast. The French navigator de Surville nearly didn't make it past Ninety Mile Beach that same year, coming close to being wrecked on a reef west of Ahipara Bay.

It has been said that the beach itself has a large enough area of white sand to happily accommodate the whole population of Auckland. The land in this region was once covered in kauri forest, but until fairly recently the beach margins were bare. The turbulent Tasman showers the shoreline with salt-laden spray, providing a stern test for even the hardiest tree. But there is now in place a programme to reclaim land from the onslaught of drifting dunes. First, native and marram grasses are planted, then lupins, and five years later seedlings of the hardy *Pinus radiata*. As a result the Aupouri State Forest now covers some 6000 hectares successfully converted from a harsh sandy environment.

The characteristic firm sands of Ninety Mile Beach occasionally double as a speedway. They were certainly put to the test by an Australian speedster, Norman 'Wizard' Smith, whose 23 hp Chrysler once smashed records on both sides of the Tasman. In 1927, after lowering his own Auckland to Wellington record of 13 hours 19 minutes by 1 hour 15 minutes, he commented that New Zealand's roads were in worse condition than on his previous visit two years earlier. Ninety Mile Beach wasn't altogether to his liking either as he failed on his attempt at the measured mile, being about 73 km/h short of the world mark. However, in 1931 he did manage a world record over 10 miles, achieving the equivalent of 264 km/h over 16 kilometres. Assistants were stationed along the beach to scare off sea birds, occupational hazards for the high speed beach motorist. 'Wizard' Smith may have become airborne at times, but there were other Australians who most certainly did. Sir Charles Kingsford Smith and Guy Menzies used Ninety Mile Beach for their trans-Tasman take-offs.

The firm sands of this beach are almost concrete-like below high-water mark. At low water on high spring tides there is an expanse of firm sand from 150 metres to nearly 300 metres wide extending for over 80 kilometres. But modern off-road motorists are urged not to emulate the 'Wizard', for sudden soft patches of

Digging for toheroas on Ninety Mile Beach. The shellfish has a memorable taste, especially when made into a soup, but nowadays you'll have to make do with tuatuas or pipis instead.

sand can be disastrous. At the other end of the speedometer, simply parking where the sand is soft and wet, or even dry and deep, can have similarly sinking results.

Ninety Mile Beach has long been popular with campers and holidaymakers, boasting robust but safe surf conditions. In fact, in 1967 it was claimed that there had not been one bathing fatality down the whole of its length in the previous 20 years. A number of fishermen were not so lucky, having being swept off the rocks. For surfers, Scott Point, at the northern end, offers a consistent 2-metre combination beach and point break, while The Bluff (near the middle of the beach) and Waipapakauri (near the southern end) are also recognised surfing spots. But when a large south swell is running, Wreck Bay at Ahipara is the place. The name honours a local landmark, the remains of the paddle steamer *Favourite* which foundered here while sheltering from a southwesterly gale in 1870.

In addition to its usual seasonal human influx, this beach once had other seasonal visitors in large numbers — in the shape of the toheroa. Unhappily, New Zealand's most coveted shellfish, the source of delicious fritters and soup, is now endangered. Overzealous hunting in the 1960s led to declining numbers and the introduction of regulations. 'Closed Season' signs went up and look like staying that way for a few years yet.

Although once plentiful on other West Coast beaches — Muriwai and near Dargaville — it was from Ahipara on Ninety Mile Beach that the toheroa got its name. A Maori war-party in desperate need of food was once ordered by a hopeful chief to dig where they saw strange slits in the sand. 'Tohe roa!' — 'persist!' — he urged them, and they did, eventually finding the succulent burrowing shellfish. And so the national dish was known thereafter as the 'toheroa'.

A relatively recent addition to the colourful history of Ninety Mile Beach is its annual four-day snapper fishing contest. For more than ten years fishermen have come from around the world to compete for big cash prizes awarded for the heaviest snapper and for the heaviest catch overall.

The contest is restricted to 1000 anglers, who come from Australia, Ireland, Scotland and Hawaii, as well as from throughout New Zealand. If evenly spaced down the considerable length of Ninety Mile Beach, each of these hopeful fishermen would have just over 100 metres of ocean each.

In view of Maori legends concerning the discovery of this country, it is hardly surprising that fishing is such a popular national pastime. The story goes that the North Island was a large fish, Te Ika-a-Maaui, hooked and 'landed' by Maaui, while the South Island was his canoe and Stewart Island its anchor. Perhaps the most surprising aspect of this exceptional catch was that Maaui's hook and the head and tail of the fish were identified as, respectively, the Mahia Peninsula,

One that didn't get away — and worth the effort of catching it.

the Wellington area and the North Auckland peninsula. Te Ika-a-Maaui appeared somewhat like a ray, its head and open mouth to the south, lengthy tail pointing north and one fin snagged by a hook. This suggests that the early Maori had an extensive knowledge of the country, long before the days of maps.

New Zealand's fascination with fish — and fishing — has a lot to do with the placement of our two main islands. Running more or less north to south they span some 13 degrees of latitude, and a considerable range of water temperatures. This is responsible for a varied list of indigenous fish, in addition to numerous other species brought here by tropical and sub-antarctic currents. It is the warm currents that bring the creatures for which New Zealand is best known by tourists – gamefish, including marlins, sharks, bonitos, tunas and albacore.

Many of these unwary specimens come to the Bay of Islands, which enjoys an international reputation as a big-game fisherman's paradise. The first official landing of a swordfish occurred there in 1913, and 11 years later the Bay of Islands Swordfish Club was formed. In 1925-26 the sport received considerable publicity from visiting American author Zane Grey, but it seems he was a lot better at penning Westerns than catching fish. Also in 1925 the sport received Royal patronage in the form of the Duke and Duchess of York, later King George VI and Queen Elizabeth. But game fishing does not necessarily involve sharks and marlin; New Zealanders are more likely to be in pursuit of the lively kingfish (or 'kingy') and kahawai.

No tale of New Zealand fish is complete without mention of the two most famous marine mammals to have graced our shores. Pelorus Jack was a friendly porpoise who regularly piloted the Picton ferry into Marlborough Sounds between 1888 and 1912. He never missed a boat, and had the added distinction of being the first dolphin in the world to be protected by law. More recently, during the summer of 1955-56, Opo the dolphin frolicked and entertained crowds of swimmers at the Hokianga beach resort of Opononi. Unfortunately Opo died by misadventure, but is honoured by a statue and a jaunty song, 'Opo the Crazy Dolphin', composed by jazz pianist Crombie Murdoch. The word 'crazy' intended no offence to Opo, being then a popular and complimentary expression.

Other inhabitants of New Zealand's coastal waters have, at times, proved much less friendly than these two remarkable animals. There has been a small number of fatalities resulting from shark attacks, and a few wounds inflicted by the barbs of sting-rays. Fishermen who haul one of the latter aboard a small boat need to steer well clear of the dangerous tail. Other monsters of the deep — not necessarily threatening — are washed ashore from time to time. Remnants of giant squid have appeared on Ninety Mile Beach, and whale strandings are unfortunately common occurrences.

In harbours and estuaries there are plenty of oppor-

tunities for the fisherman with a small boat. Large kingfish can be caught relatively close to shore, as can kahawai and the most popular — and edible — prize of all, snapper.

Back on the land, an endless supply of beaches provides an easier — and no doubt safer — alternative. Vast stocks of shellfish and other natural feed entice other sea creatures to our coast, and for these the surfcaster needs only a rod, sunhat and patience. Junior beachgoers require even less equipment, of course, for the inspection of rock and tidal pools for crabs and other members of the crustacean and molluscan families.

Every fisherman is expected to have a favourite and well-honed tall tale about 'the one that got away'. The varied nature of New Zealand's coast almost guarantees a healthy supply of colourful and fairly believable anecdotes. And to prove that the big ones don't always get away, consider the story of the Gore doctor who landed a two-metre long shark armed only with a cricket bat. Preparing to bowl in a friendly game of beach cricket, the doctor interrupted the game to wade into the water with a cricket bat after his son had spotted the shark swimming close by. After dealing a couple of attacking shots to the animal the doctor pulled it ashore by the tail. The local surf club was not impressed: 'There is a procedure to deal with these things,' an official stated, 'and it does not include wading into the water with a cricket bat.'

Hoping for a bite.

In 1964 one writer suggested that if the English are known as a nation of shopkeepers, then New Zealanders deserved to go down in history as a nation of handymen. This was on account of the local ability to knock up a bach — albeit of a fairly basic construction. This do-it-yourself skill (which the same writer claimed was inherited from the pioneers) was a rare quality which ensured New Zealand an architectural genre of its own.

The essential bach is a simple structure, traditionally of either timber, Fibrolite and corrugated iron, or combinations of those elements. Its early development was actually encouraged by local authorities' interpretations of the Housing Improvement Act of 1945. The latter was designed to ensure a certain standard of living, and defined a 'house' to be 'a building, tent, caravan, or other structure or erection, whether permanent or temporary, which is used ... in whole or in part for human habitation ... '.

The humble bach has at times also found itself in the vanguard of suburbanisation. In the 1940s and 1950s, for instance, these home-made retreats were scattered along the northern bays of Auckland's then sparsely populated 'Hibiscus Coast'. With the advent of the city's Harbour Bridge in the latter part of the fifties, what were once beach resorts became dormitory suburbs.

Many other coastal communities have had similar experiences: Raumati, some 50 kilometres from Wellington, began life as a characteristic bach settlement. Today it is a residential suburb of the capital. Similarly, New Brighton and Sumner have been assimilated by the spread of urban Christchurch. Indeed, the beach has been a powerful influence on New Zealand's demographics and town development. Alongside such specialised stimuli as railway and hydro-electric construction, mineral extraction and forestry, is the seemingly magnetic attraction of the sea.

Times change and so do baches. Strictly speaking, 'bach' is an inappropriate description of many holiday homes now found beside our beaches. Rather it is the 'classic' bach that made its appearance during the twenty years or so following the Second World War that interests us here. 'Baching' is logically derived

A proud icon of the New Zealand coast — do-it-yourself architecture.

from 'bachelor', implying a man alone surviving under basic conditions. This led to the 'bach', but that shelter at the beach was never just a bachelor's retreat. It was a haven for the whole family, where life took on a more casual aspect and was spared such tiresome intrusions as school and work. Its primary philosophy was simplicity, and was an eagerly anticipated contrast with home life. Here, meals were fairly informal and nobody got into too much trouble for bringing sand inside.

Some baches may have bordered on the primitive, but that was their conscious charm. Certainly — in earlier days anyway — there seemed little point in a slavish duplication of city domesticity at the beach. The bach therefore became a handy retirement home for furniture and fittings that had already done their dash. It has been suggested that one of the great advantages of baches is the pressure they take off secondhand shops and auction houses, these businesses being eternally grateful for not having to absorb all of the nation's cast-off washtubs and mangles, for example. At the beach such items can, however, take on a new lease of life, providing facilities for, respectively, rinsing salt-laden togs and winching boats.

As for first impressions, the quintessential bach was pretty straightforward, not usually bothered with sophisticated architectural details. The main requirement was probably a generous number of windows on the seaward side to take in the view, surely one of the bach's main reasons for being. This vista — and associated sound effects — could be enjoyed from the comfort of a window seat, divan or old sofa, with piles of well-worn magazines and paperbacks at the ready.

If the bach was on a sloping section its underside doubled as handy storage for beach equipment, boats and the like. Odd lengths of timber and spare windows might also be filed away there, just in case of future running repairs.

It was usual for the bach to share its section with two other essential structures, the water tank and

The humble bach: its principal philosophy was simplicity.

dunny. The first took the run-off from the roof and stood elevated on a wooden framework. In many instances this construction predated treated timber and so needed regular attention, and was also under constant attack from rising kikuyu grass. A handy stick may have been used to thump its corrugations to determine the current water level, and such tanks were often the source of demise for inquisitive opossums and other wildlife.

The toilet or dunny, on the other hand, was a 'long drop' arrangement, comfortably distanced from the bach proper, and distinguished by a front door which opened to reveal all. A more 'civilised' bach of this era may have enjoyed the comparative luxury of a septic tank and a toilet that could be incorporated into the main structure.

Around the rest of the section grew grass, of sorts. The first chore of any holiday was to beat the growth into submission with the motor mower, and that was probably it for the summer, unless anyone could be particularly bothered. A popular addition to the section was a crushed shell path, perhaps bordered by beach boulders, white-washed or picked out in bold primaries.

Indeed, when it came to colour schemes, bach owners often exercised considerable imagination. The muted shades demanded of suburbia were happily replaced with decidedly tropical or Caribbean colours, such choices possibly influenced by the economics of discounted hardware shop remnants. Nevertheless, a paint mixing error on the part of the retailer was put to advantage, brightening up the New Zealand coast. Whatever the hue, a 'must' with bach paint concerned its application: that is, it went on much thicker than usual. House painting is a little envied task, and particularly so at the beach. The occasional 'touch up', therefore, demanded a good, quick coverage, though this desirable viscosity was often unavoidable anyway owing to the old paint solidifying in the tin.

At the door of the bach was an assortment of discarded jandals and beach equipment: fishing rods fought for space with dripping togs and towels. Any sand tramped inside quickly got disguised by a horrendously coloured and patterned carpet square or two. Furniture was decidedly casual, and at the mercy of a free-flow of holidaymakers. The aim of the bach may have been to get away from it all, but on the patio or down on the sand, a transistor kept one in touch with the latest racing or cricket results.

Bach decor was based on basic linings, often painted hardboard with patterned wallpaper for additional accent. The lounge wall may have been relieved only by a calendar from the local dairy or garage, the essential tide chart and a bookshelf invariably well-stocked with Reader's Digest condensations and a ragged assortment of family games, Monopoly money intermixed with playing cards.

The main activity occurred around the dining table, perhaps a tubular steel and formica set retired from home and, at meal times, invariably this was laid with a ragged assortment of crockery — probably Crown Lynn — and mismatched cutlery. Above all this was the ceiling, routinely sagging 8 foot by 4 foot panels of Pinex, their ragged edges cunningly concealed by battens.

Basic baches varied according to the tastes and resources of their owners, but one common feature was their atmosphere, particularly after being closed up for a period. Kapok mattresses, camp stretchers, old wire-woves and bedding somehow combined to produce an aroma — and, unfortunately for hay-fever sufferers, a source of dust — characteristic of the New Zealand bach.

If there is one building material traditionally associated with baches it is the mineral fibre cement sheet, or Fibrolite, as it was generally known. Consisting of a mixture of asbestos fibre and Portland cement, it came in sheets up to 10 feet long and 4 feet wide. Its appeal for the walls of baches was its economy and ease of installation, not to mention — according to the manufacturer — its elegance. It *was* certainly rot- and borer-proof, and possibly fire-proof, as well as being easy to paint, so was ideally suited for the maintenance-free bach. It also came in corrugated form for roofing, and was no doubt more resistant to the ravages of salt-laden air than standard roofing iron.

'Asbestos-cement sheeting' was a bit of a mouthful, so the material was generally known by the tradename 'Fibrolite', much to the pleasure of its Australian makers, James Hardie & Co. But there was another earlier brand on the market, Poilite, imported from England.

There were a couple of tricks to the installation of Fibrolite. Firstly, sheets were either cut with a guillotine or scored with an old file and snapped over a straight length of 4 x 2. Secondly, blunt-headed nails were essential for fixing. Once up, joints between sheets were covered with battens or mouldings, of timber, metal or more mineral fibre cement. However, Fibrolite is now a material of the past, a relic of the days when builders were blissfully oblivious to the dangers of asbestos.

A design for a 'simple but practical' beach retreat was offered in the *Weekly News* in 1964. It was an

'You shall know them by their water tanks...'

The foreshore at Castor Bay in Auckland in the 1900s. Later years would see this beach and others on Auckland's North Shore dotted with baches, the advance guard of 'suburbs in the sand'.

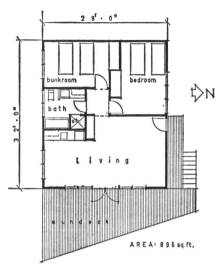

example of an 'unpretentious bach, having the merit of practical informality coupled with good utilisation of space'. If the proposed section was flat, all the aspiring bach owner had to do was lay a slab of concrete and knock up the framing in 4 x 2. The rest was supposed to be as simple as the bach lifestyle itself.

Examination of the plan reveals a genius for simplicity. The suggested dimensions were 32 feet by 28 feet — both handy multiples of 4 feet. So that if standard sheets of Fibrolite were used, there would be little wastage. The recommended living space took up nearly half the total floor area, commanding a 270-degree view, and extended on to a sundeck. The parents' bedroom was positioned in the north-west corner to catch both the view and afternoon sun, while the kids' bunkroom managed only a bit of the latter. The compact kitchen and bathroom facilities were back-to-back, to economise on plumbing.

The history of New Zealand's baches is a rich tale of recycling and building in peculiar places. Many of the first baches were built from the likes of used car cases which, being constructed of hardwoods like cedar, have proved durable. Old trams have also been put to good use, as has the occasional cave. So that for any self-respecting bach, recent trends in holiday housing must be alarming. Whereas baches were once happiest when modest and improvised, nowadays they are professionally constructed with sealed drives to their doors. In our progress, some of the spirit of the old bach has been lost. Those pockets of authentic, quirky bach constructions which still exist will, with luck, continue to defy the elements and add a dash of Kiwi to our enjoyment of the beach.

BEACH UMB

To brighten up yo or fold up for carr shelter at Beach. 72 inches diameter, all complete wit

No. 61: Good qu Duck (Red ar Blue and White

No. 71: Fadeless Duck.

No. 19 FOLDING

A very comfortable chair of ample propor exceptional comfort; m a standard Deck chair required. Not varnish

Folds flat in one mo

Covered in "Special" qu canvas only

Footrest extra

For many New Zealanders, the beach holiday is a regular summer ritual, often at the same beach year after year.

There can be few beach views as spectacular as that of Piha near Auckland from the top of the road before its final descent to the coastal flat. This introduction, and the promise of a fortnight in the sun, entices many Aucklanders back there every year. Such was once the case with the Hamilton family.

In 1953 they had come from Reading, England, to settle in suburban Howick, on the southern shores of Auckland's Waitemata Harbour. But life near Howick Beach did not compare with the excitement of an annual holiday at Piha.

Nowadays the Piha road is sealed all the way, but not so in the mid fifties. Lacking a car, the Hamiltons took the bus to downtown Auckland, changing to the Piha connection and one and a half hours' travel on mostly shingle roads. Two weeks away at the beach called for much preparation, including cartons of bedding and provisions, especially fresh vegetables not available at the Piha store. A fifth family member regularly made the journey, illegally. The family sausage dog travelled to the beach year after year, secreted in a hold-all bag. The bus journey was a loathsome one, the young holdaymakers in the family suffering from a mixture of travel sickness and anticipation.

In later years the Hamiltons had transport of their own, a sky blue Ford Prefect which made the trip to the

Lion Rock, Piha, 1948.

West Coast more direct, but not necessarily more comfortable. Pamela, older sister Sabrina and the dog were confined to the back seat, along with those bits of fishing tackle that couldn't be tied to the roof. The car regularly boiled, necessitating a stop near the Waiatarua fire station for a top-up with water which was carried for such an emergency.

The girls started planning their summer wardrobes, especially for the Surf Club dance on New Year's Eve, as soon as school had broken up. Bikinis were made (it was now the 1960s) and there were matching shorts and tops, the latter with dangling bobbles at the midriff. Shorts were Bermuda-style, with white string waistbands. Jandals were essential, but there were no sunhats: only white zinc ointment to discourage burning, and calamine lotion to soothe it.

A highlight of the journey to the beach was the first glimpse of Piha from the Lookout, and a stop was always made for this dress circle view of surf-fringed Lion Rock. It was a preview of the long-awaited holiday, but also gave the girls the chance to assess the local camping ground. A good turn-out of tents increased the likelihood of young males.

First stop were the cabins — now gone — below the road on the descent into Piha. Each unit had two sets of bunks, a single-element stove, no hot water, and smelled of Sunlight soap and Chemico cleanser. There was a plastic fly curtain on the door, a handy fly swat for those that got in, and a communal long-drop.

The Piha break began after Christmas Day and usually benefited from the Christmas presents: usually such items as lilos and plastic beach bags with drawstrings and pictures of hula girls and palm trees. Beach towels, striped and with fringing, completed the kit. Much time was spent teasing up the hair, hence a reluctance to get it wet, and the primary activity was observing the boys, usually at the store and from behind a milkshake.

Pamela's Piha holidays with the family lasted until the late sixties, the beach providing a gradual initiation into adult life. There were annual get-togethers, picture shows and dances, and the camping ground where the boys whistled at the two sisters.

New Zealanders can claim a long association with life under canvas. The early European arrivals here often resorted to shelters either improvised from local materials, or from items carried with them. The latter naturally enough included tents, or at least sheets of canvas, these shelters frequently pitched in sufficient numbers to create temporary 'canvas towns' which sheltered explorers, goldminers and bushmen throughout the most rugged reaches of the country. In time the tent made the transition to recreational use, no doubt encouraged by such pursuits as boy scouting.

A holiday camp among the sand dunes at Paraparaumu Beach, 1914.

them were ridge tents, touring tents and squat tents, made of calico, canvas and duck. There was also a motorist's tent which accommodated campers and their car as well. Inside, the comfortable camper needed rubber ground sheets, collapsible canvas beds, a meths-burning portable stove, hurricane lamp for emergencies and, of course, a quick-boiling Thermette — promising 12 cups of tea in 5 minutes under any conditions.

Twenty years later and the serious camper may have had a 'sturdily-made family tent' to pitch 'on a convenient roadside spot wherever nightfall finds you'. With brown duck walls and a green waterproof roof it was also resistant to damaging mildew. Further, it had ventilators in the roof and tent flaps that could be extended for coolness and shade. Rubber lilos now ensured a more comfortable night's sleep, and a wide range of adjustable and folding camp stools and chairs — including the Rotorua chair (39/6) with striped canvas and wide arm rests — encouraged a lot of just 'taking it easy'.

In the early days of camping in New Zealand it was simply a matter of selecting a suitable spot. But by

The outdoor life in New Zealand received a major boost from the 1925 South Seas Exhibition in Dunedin. Camping facilities were constructed for visitors, many of whom enjoyed the novel accommodation and took it up on an annual basis. By the end of that decade the Farmers' Union Trading Company of Auckland was stocking the Reliable tent, suitable 'as an auxiliary to the home, as a summer-house, or for holiday purposes'. Locally made 'to suit colonial requirements' it had the added advantage of 'hand-worked grummets'.

By the early 1930s an extensive range of tents was available to the adventurous New Zealander. Among

the middle of the present century and a whole generation familiar with the outdoor life, a bit of organisation had become necessary. For reasons of health, specific areas of coastal locales were set aside leading to the large number of camping grounds now found throughout the country.

Modern camping exponents do not need to take quite as much equipment as the pioneers, for many sites now offer extensive amenities. Camp shops provide fresh supplies of bread, milk and newspapers, and there's often a communal recreational centre in which sociable campers can play games, watch TV or just mingle. In addition, there may be a nearby beach store of the emporium kind still to be run across which stocks everything from fish hooks to books and vegetables.

Summer it may be, but the elements can be decidedly unseasonable and unpredictable. The weather at Christmas and New Year can be bad enough to confine campers to their tents for days on end, necessitating emergency drainage manoeuvres — the hasty excavation of trenches to divert the downpour away from tent sites — and some real resourcefulness in the entertainment area to avoid mutiny, if not homicide.

By mid January the first wave of residents is returning to work, shortly to be replaced by a wave of older campers who prefer the quieter life, patiently awaiting the departure of families. These folk will, in addition, usually enjoy the more settled weather that tends to prevail through February and March.

Camping isn't for everyone, being something of an acquired art. Those introduced to it at an early age may happily carry on the annual tradition, but others cannot be bothered with its primitive charm. For some, in fact, the New Zealand camping ground is viewed as the ultimate horror. Others may agree but suggest that, if so, at least it is *our* ultimate horror.

'... **blending together in a happy confusion of jandals, shorts, T-shirts and togs.**'

Rather than an overseas version, as the late John Collins contemplated in a piece entitled 'Hot Enough for You, Mate?' for the Christchurch *Press* in the 1970s. It had been suggested that the British resort company, Butlins, could be interested in setting up camp here:

'Of course, we had been thoroughly briefed by senior Butlin's Redcoats about what to expect and had had access to aerial photographs showing the layout of a typical camp, but all the training in the world would not have been enough to stop my stomach turning at the stench of boil-in-the-bag curries and tinned spaghetti-with-sausages that met me as I stopped the vehicle at the main entrance.

Kitchen duty at Paraparaumu during the summer of 1954.

' "She's Right Macht Frei", the camp's ghoulishly ironic motto, was emblazoned in broken beer bottles on the side of the camp commandant's quarters. I jumped from the jeep and walked boldly in, expecting at least some resistance. Too late. Anticipating our advance, he had chosen their usual way out: he lay slumped over the desk clutching a "No Vacancy" sign and surrounded by empty brown bottles. Anger welled up in me as I saw displayed around the walls the instruments of his vile trade — plastic tikis, opossum slippers, place mats with views of the alps, machine-turned Maori carvings, bumper stickers, and other horrifying excesses of a civilisation gone mad.

'The air seemed horribly oppressive, and I walked outside, blinking in the bright light. So this was the instrument of the final holiday solution: a New Zealand motor camp. A tall black chimney belching clouds of burnt toast and cries of "This bloody plug's gone again" told me where the notorious kitchen block lay, but I felt too sick to face it. I wandered the compound, unsure of how the inmates, some of whom had been there for more than a week, would react. I can still see the blank, uncomprehending looks on their faces, the poor creatures, as I tried to communicate with them.

' "Good morning, I'm from Butlin's Holiday Camps advance force of Redcoats. Don't worry, my man, you'll be all right," I said to a typical unfortunate. His body was horribly bloated, the swollen gut lying in folds over the waistband of the regulation-issue, drip-dry, calf-length walk shorts. He allowed his blistered, peeling face to crack into a grisly simulacrum of a grin.

' "G'day," he replied from under the orange towelling hat all the inmates wore. "Hot enough for you?"

'I moved on. His mind had obviously gone. It was the same with the others. Whenever I greeted one of them and tried to explain my purpose, the regimented greeting would be chanted, various in form but always on the same theme: "She's a hot one, all right" or "Good weather for a few chilled ones", or "She's a bloody ripper today".

'I left them insanely tinkering with their outboard motors, struggling with their candy-striped awnings, or vainly attempting to drive tent pegs into the glacial moraines on which the camps were always built.

'The women were if anything even more pitiful. Like the men they were red, bloated, peeling, and demented about the weather, but — perhaps because of their concern for the children or because at least some of them were sober — they seemed less resigned than the men to this way of life. They still pathetically believed the rumours that constantly circulated in this sort of camp that a functioning washing machine had been unearthed or that someone had repaired the fuses in the kitchen. It was heart-rending to see their frenzied rush, pushing and struggling, whenever someone finished with the toaster.

'Bloodcurdling screams drifted from the shower block. Some unfortunate had been lured in with the promises of a warm shower and was even now struggling with the temperature control as alternate jets of freezing and scalding water blasted him. Even children and pregnant women were not immune to this foul torture.

'The beach was sickening, even to one who had once visited Brighton. The camp administrators had not had the time to cover up their misdeeds, and the shore was littered with steaming salmon-pink bodies in various states of corpulence and neglect. Occasionally, in response to a weird whistling noise from the radio, the oiled bodies would unstick themselves from the sand and turn over, muttering incoherent comments to the effect that she was indeed a hot one.

'Well, thank Sir Billy, that day was years ago now, and the world knows the full horrors of the final holiday solution, the insane attempt to create a week's holiday that would seem as if it had lasted a thousand years: and of how Butlin's were given the job of putting New Zealanders on the right road.

'Sitting here, huddled behind the windbreak in my deck-chair on the imported chilled-gravel beach and watching the holiday-makers in their ex-R.A.F. blazers, handkerchiefs neatly knotted on their heads, flannels rolled to just below the knee, bucket, spade, and Dennis Wheatley novels in their hands, I can feel proud that Britain, for all her lost empire, has finally shown the colony the civilised way to holiday.'

Acknowledgements

The authors are grateful to the following individuals and organisations for information and for making available various textual and pictorial materials. A detailed illustrations list appears below. Every effort has been made to trace the copyright owners of the material used in this book. The authors apologise for any omissions from the following list and will be pleased to hear from those they were unable to trace.

Mrs Grace Adams; Virginia Addison; Alexander Turnbull Library; Auckland Maritime Museum; Auckland Public Library; Anna Blackman (for permission to quote material from her article on Dunedin's St Clair Salt Water Baths); Christine Brown; Canterbury Museum; Canterbury Society of Arts; City of Napier; the late John Collins; CSA Gallery; Dunedin City Council; the J. E. Farrelly Collection; Cecilie Geary; Gisborne District Council; Grey District Council; Penny Hansen; Hocken Library; Helen Humphries; Duncan Mackay; Robert McDougall Art Gallery; David McGill; Fiona McKergow (for permission to quote information from her article 'Bodies at the Beach: A History of Swimwear'); Dorothy Murray; City of Napier; National Museum; New Plymouth District Council; *New Zealand Herald*; Heather Nicholson; Ron Palenski; South Canterbury Museum; Sumner-Redcliffs Historical Society; Tauranga District Council; Paul Thompson; Waitaki District Council; Wanganui District Council; Wellington City Council; Whakatane District Museum; Whangarei District Council; Penny Whiting; Wilson & Horton Ltd; Pam Wolfe.

Illustration Credits

The following list identifies the copyright ownership and the source of photographs. Those photographs not specifically identified are from the collections of the authors.

Abbreviations:
- t = top
- b = bottom
- l = left
- r = right

- APL = Auckland Public Library
- ATL = Alexander Turnbull Library
- CM = Canterbury Museum
- HL = Hocken Library
- NM = National Museum
- NZH = New Zealand Herald

Front cover photograph NZH; **back cover photograph** NZH; **page 5** ATL; **6** Mrs Grace Adams and CSA Gallery; **8** ATL J. & M. Daley Coll.; **9** ATL; **11** CM (6969); **12** *Punch* magazine; **13** (t) *Punch* magazine, (b) HL (E650/10); **14** (t) CM (6969), (b)

ATL F. G. Radcliffe Coll. (G6364½); **15** ATL (857¼); **17** ATL *Christchurch Press* Coll. (41281½); **18** ATL Price Coll. (458½); **19** ATL (C17676); **20** ATL Curry Coll. (F53140½); **21** *Weekly News* (1904); **22** (l) CM *Lyttleton Times* Coll. (2215½), (r) ATL Ephemera; **23** NM; **24** ATL (49155½); **25** Sumner-Redcliffs Historical Society; **26** (r) ATL Ephemera; **27** all photographs NZH; **29** ATL Tesla Coll. (G16442 1/1); **30** ATL Waihi Arts Centre Coll. (F116723½); **31** ATL F. G. Radcliffe Coll. (G6253½); **32** (l) *Weekly News*, (r) NZH; **33** (t) CM (7626), (b) ATL Hunter-Brown Coll. (F13247 1/1); **34** ATL Tesla Coll. (G16442 1/1); **35** ATL (F152880½); **36** (t) ATL Collis Coll. (G21363½), (b) ATL Making New Zealand Coll. (F222MNZ½); **37** ATL (G100634½); **38** (t) *Weekly News;* **39** NZH; **40** NZH; **41** NZH; **42-3** NZH; **43** (r) NZH; **44** both photographs J. E. Farrelly Coll.; **45** (b) NZH; **46** NZH; **47** NZH; **48** ATL 1/2. Hall-Raine Coll. (G100663½); **49** NZH; **50** (t) ATL F. N. Jones Coll. (G26278½), (b) APL (A1367); **51** (b) ATL E. T. Robson Coll. (C17789); **53** ATL Gordon Burt Coll. (G36931½); **54** *Punch* magazine (1897); **55** ATL (1876½); **56** ATL Steffano Webb Coll. (G9066 1/1); **57** ATL F. N. Jones Coll. (G28885½); **58** ATL Gordon Burt Coll. (F15419 1/1); **59** ATL *Christchurch Press* Coll. (G40809½); **60** (l) Punch magazine (1913); **61** ATL Gordon Burt Coll. (G36931½); **62** (l-r) ATL Schmidt Coll. (G1863 1/1), ATL (C17674), ATL Gordon Burt Coll. (G36931½), (unknown), NZH; **63** ATL National Publicity Studios Coll. (F27528½); **64** NZH; **65** ATL (F126064½); **66** NZH; **67** ATL; **68** ATL J. D. Pascoe Coll. (F1947¼); **69** (t) ATL National Publicity Studios Coll. (F27530½), (b) ATL; **71** ATL (G21524½); **73** (l) HL (5011), (r) NZH; **74** ATL S. C. Smith Coll. (G47673½); **75** CM (2111); **76** *Weekly News;* **77** (l) ATL (C17680), (r) ATL National Archives (126108½); **78** ATL F. N. Jones Coll. (G32896½); **79** ATL Ephemera; **80** (tl) ATL Ephemera (C17678), (tr) ATL Ephemera (C17677), (b) ATL S. C. Smith Coll. (G46398½); **81** ATL Price Coll. (C17872); **82** NZH; **83** NZH; **84** ATL Watt Coll. (80560½); **85** ATL J. McAllister Coll. (G7966 1/1); **86** (l) *Weekly News;* **87** (l) ATL Ephemera (C17673), (c) ATL Ephemera (C17670); **88** ATL National Publicity Studios Coll. (F27457½); **89** NZH; **91** ATL (G21524½); **92** ATL Jeffares Coll. (G76449½); **93** ATL National Publicity Studios Coll. (F27453½); **95** NZH; **97** ATL Northwood Coll. (G10903½); **98** ATL (F75567½); **99** NZH; **100** NZH; **101** NZH; **102** Paul Thompson; **103** all photographs Paul Thompson; **104** NZH; **106** NZH; **107** ATL Price Coll. (1627½); **108** (l) *Weekly News;* **109** ATL National Publicity Studios Coll. (F33097½); **112** ATL G. H. Howell Coll. (F71003½); **113** NZH; **114** NZH; **120** ATL.

Index

Bold numbers indicate an illustrative reference

Ahipara 96, 99
ambergris 46
Aupouri Peninsula 96
Aupouri State Forest 97
Awana beach 45

bach 102-108, **102**, **103**, **104**, **106**
bathing, mixed 22-3
bathing caps 23, 57, 58
bathing machine 13-14, **13**, **14**
Bay of Plenty 92-6
beachcombing 46-8
beauty contests 68-9, **69**, 75-6, **76**
Bethells Beach 45
Blenheim 76, 77
the Bluff 99
boating 50
Brophys Beach 90
buckets and spades 36, **36**, 38
Buffalo Beach 90

camping 111-5, **112**, **113**, **114**
Cape Egmont 45
Cape Foulwind **81**
Cape Reinga 96
Cape Runaway 84
Caroline Bay **14**, 69, 72-6, **73**, 86
Castlecliff 45

Castor Bay **107**
Cathedral Cove 90
Cave Rock beach **14**
Clifton Bay **25**
coastal roads 33, **33**, 35-6
Collingwood 79
Collins, John 114
Colville 92
Cooks Beach 90
Cooks Cove 84
Coromandel Peninsula 88-92
the Cut 79

Dargaville 47, 99
Days Bay **37**

East Coast 83-4, 86
Eastbourne 45
Eastern Beach **39**
Evans Bay **80**

Farewell Spit 79
Farmers' Trading Company 58, **58**, **61**
Fibrolite 102, 106, 108
fishing 99-101
Fletchers Bay 92
Front Beach **91**

Garston 7
Gisborne 77, 84, 86
Glinks Gully 47
Golden Bay **33**, 77, 79
Goose Bay **82**

Hahei beach **89**
Hibiscus Coast 102
Hicks Bay 83, 84
Hikurangi 83
Hotwater Beach 90
Houghton Bay 45
Howick Beach 109
Huhuwai 83
Hyde, Robin 94

jandals 37, 110,

Kaikoura 82
Kaiteriteri 79
Kaitohe beach 45
Kenepuru 82
Kennedys Bay 92
Kingsford Smith, Sir Charles 97

Laidlaw Leeds 57, 58
Lake Taupo 45
Ligar Bay 79

lilo 37-38, **38**
Lion Rock **109**
Lonely Beach 90
Lyall Bay 25, 45

Mahia Peninsula 45, 99
Makorori 45, 86
Mangamaunu 82
Maori Bay 45
Marahau 79
Marfell Beach 82
Marlborough Sounds 79, 100
Matarangi Beach 90
Matata 45
Maunganui Bluff 48
Medlands beach 45
Mellons Bay **46**
Menzies, Guy 97
Mercury Bay 90
Midway 86
Milford 45
Moruriki Island 96
Motueka 79
Mount Maunganui (The Mount) 45, 69, 83, 93-6, **93**, **95**,
Murdoch, Crombie 100
Muriwai 45, 99
Music 40-1, **40**

Napier **77, 84**
Nelson 76, 77, 78-9
New Brighton **6**, 45, **59**, 102
New Brighton Pier **75**
Ngamotu Beach **36**, 85
Ninety Mile Beach 36, 46, 96-9, **97**, **98**, **99**, 100, **101**

Oakura 41
Ocean Beach (Dunedin) **22**
Ohope 45, 96
Omanu 45
Onerahi **31**
Opo 100
Opononi 100
Opotiki 45, 83, 96
Opoutere 89
Orewa 45
Oriental Bay **66**
Otaki Health Camp **68**
Otama Beach 90

P class (yacht) 50-1, **51**
  Harry Highet 50-1, **51**
Pakawau 79
Papamoa 96
Paraparaumu Beach **112**, 114
Partons Rock 79
Pauanui 89
Pelorus Jack 100
picnicking 30-3, **32, 34, 35, 47, 48, 49**
Piha 41, 45, 109-11, **109**
Pilot Bay 94
Plunket Society 67
Pohara 79

Port Charles 92
postcards **22, 80**
Pouawa 84
Poverty Bay 86, 93
Puponga 79

Queen Charlotte Sound 82

Rabbit Island 79
Raglan 43
Raumati 102
Red Beach 45
Rings Beach 90
Riwaka 76
Ruby Bay 79

St Clair **13**, 14, 45, **74**
St Clair Salt Water Baths 14, 15
St Kilda **23**, 45,
Sandy Bay 79
Scarborough 45
Scott Point 99
Sears, Roebuck Catalogue **55,56**
sharks, danger of 20-1
Smith, Norman 'Wizard' 97
Sumner **25**, **33**, 45, 102
sunbathing 65-8
Sunlight League **65**
surf boards **41**, 42, 43, **43**, 44
surf life-saving 25, **25, 26, 27**
surf life-saving clubs and associations:
  Bondi 25
  Castlecliff 25
  Lyall Bay 25, 26
  Maranui 26

New Brighton 25
New Zealand Surf Life-Saving Association 26
Sumner **25**
surfing 41-45, **41**, **42-3**, 78, 79, 88, 89, 94
  beaches 43-5
  New Zealand Surfboard Riders Association 42
swimming, how to 15-16
  at the beach 16-7, 19-21
swimsuits **22, 24,** 54-64,
  bikini **62, 64, 64**
  Canadian costume 24, 25, 55, **55**, 57, **57, 62**
  Canterbury 62
  Jantzen **61**
  neck-to-knee 54-5
  regulations governing 22, 24-5, 54
  Roslyn 60, 62
  Speedo 60
  two-piece **62**, 62, **64**

Tahunanui (Tahuna) **78**, 79
Tainui 89
Tairua Harbour 89
Takapuna beach **18**, 45
Tapu 92
Taranaki 44
Tata Beach 79
Tatapouri 84
Tauranga 93
Tauwaiwe Stream 90
Te Araroa 83, 84
Te Kaha 83

The Portage 82
Thermette 32, **32**, 112
Timaru 72
Titahi Bay **48**
toheroa **97**, 99
Tokomaru Bay 84
Tokoroa Point 89
Tolaga Bay 84
Totaranui 79

Waihau Bay 84
Waihi 45, 88, 96
Waihi Beach **30**, 88
Waikanae 45, 86
Waikareao Estuary 93
Waikato Heads 45
Waikawau Bay 92
Waimapu Estuary 93
Wainui Beach 45, 86
Waiotahi 83
Waipapakauri 99
Waipu Cove **76**
Wellington **80**
Whakatane 96
Whangamata 45, 89, 90
Whangamata Bar 89
Whangamata Beach 89
Whangamata Estuary 89
Whangaparaoa Bay 84
Whangara 84
Wharekaho Bay (Simpsons Beach) 90
Whiritoa 89
Whitianga 45, 90, **91**
Wreck Bay 99